Dream Palaces

Dream Palaces

FANTASTIC HOUSES
AND THEIR TREASURES

Claude Arthaud

THAMES AND HUDSON · LONDON

Published in Great Britain in 1973 by
Thames and Hudson Ltd, London

First published in French under the title *Les Palais du Rêve*
© B. Arthaud and Paris-Match, Paris
This edition © 1972 by Claude Arthaud

Printed in France

ISBN 0 500 34056 0

Contents

Enchanted Visions

Contents

Introduction

The palaces described in this book belong to a world of wonder. The need for beauty and perfection created them, sometimes at the price of naïveté. If, in the theater, the false is truer than the real, these residences of wonder, which perhaps seem false in reality, seem right in relation to the dreams which preceded them. The castles of Ludwig II of Bavaria reflect his yearning for the unattainable. Linderhof, Neuschwanstein, and Herrenchiemsee were dreams dreamed, coveted, and realized. But such palaces, no longer the stuff of dreams, need a justification for their existence. Their beauty is at the mercy of their unreason. One may wish to see them or ignore them. They may delight or repel. Art is not always a factor in their making. How, then, does their magic fail, so that even the force of the dream is in question? The failure lies in the utter simplicity of the visions which produced them. Cinderella's pumpkin can become a coach, but the quality of the pumpkin and the coach are never in dispute. What matters is the metamorphosis from dream to reality, from the house dreamed to the house built.

The people who wanted such places almost all believed they were building them for an ideal, out of love, even if this were self-love (which is after all one of love's facets). But grand passions have generally been experienced in more commonplace settings. These dream palaces, like the gilded cradles of their creators, weighed down with too much hope, were fatal to the dreamers. Neither Ludwig II of Bavaria, nor Beckford, nor Marie Antoinette, nor the Princess de Lamballe preserved their follies any more than the gilded cradles of the King of Rome or of Henri IV of France could preserve them from their tragic destinies. There might be a moral here, if we did not know that in times without follies

Enchanted Visions

unattainable dreams are a necessity. They would have to be invented if they did not exist. It has been proved that a cat whose brain has been damaged in such a way that it has lost its capacity to dream will shortly die. Nobody has dared say this of man, but for the owners of these palaces it was dreaming which, after bringing them to life, killed them. The majority died beheaded, exiled, or ruined, condemned for dreaming in lonely defiance of contemporary society. Their dreams were misanthropic, while the cost of their follies always exceeded their own resources or those of the state. Time has passed, the dreamers are dead, and their dwellings have crumbled; some of these dwellings are still visited, but many have been forgotten.

The quality of wonder in the buildings presented here is harmless compared with the fantastic character of some other edifices and merely reflects the pursuit of the agreeable and beautiful. The follies disappear and, with them, the dream palaces. Society often knows nothing about them, and the poets will never have enough power to protect them. Neither André Breton, Paul Éluard, Colette, Pieyre de Mandiargues, nor Salvador Dali have succeeded in rescuing the aedicules and the truncated column of the "Desert" of Retz, a few miles from Paris. The forest is completing the process of destruction. Soon there will be nothing left.

One is tempted to classify these dreams by nation, race, and type. And why can we not judge a country's imagination by its dreams and the palaces which they inspired, and not simply by its painting, literature, and music?

If one judges the spirit of a people by its wit and humor, one might equally judge it by its dream palaces, visionaries, and eccentrics, and assess the contribution of a nation's dreamers. These are more numerous in some countries than in others. Are there any rules? There are more dream palaces and people who execute their fantasies in the Saxon, Nordic, and Germanic lands than in Latin countries, except in Italy, where sixteenth-century humanism was overtaken by a mannerist movement more concerned with man's vagaries than his stability. This saved Italy from rationalism.

There are more witches and apparitions in Shakespeare's world, and more dream palaces in England than anywhere else. The reef that can be taken for the coast can also be taken for a keep. Seen from a distance, Scotland's granite peaks are almost indistinguishable from her castles. Why should castles not assume the misty forms of phantasmagoria?

Religions, too, exercise a modifying influence on national imagination. By exasperating some of its detractors, puritanism in England created social outcasts, often rich and intelligent men, and drove them into spectacular conflict with society. Accused of nameless crimes for having shut himself in his mother's mansion with his cousin Louisa and the young Lord Courtenay for three days and nights at Christmas, William Beckford was to exorcise the scandal by writing *Vathek*, a masterpiece of Romanticism. This sublimation of impropriety was to influence the entire satanic school of the nineteenth century, from Byron to Poe and Baudelaire. The subsequent erection of Fonthill Abbey's crazy towers was an exile's gesture of defiance against the society that had rejected him.

The lands bathed by the North and Baltic Seas are no less adorned by Oriental pagodas than England. The Chinese palace of Drottningholm and the metal tents of Haga in Sweden are royal instances of a distinctive architecture commonly found in this region in the eighteenth century.

Enchanted Visions

The forests of Bavaria and Austria and the ancient possessions of German princes may be what the mists are to Scandinavia. Just as the mists engulf the landscape and deceive the eyes, so the enveloping vegetation dissolves men's reason and disintegrates their vision. The myths and legends of the woods suggest an infinity of symbolic combinations and transmutations. Man becomes tree or animal, Actæon a stag, while Saint Hubert's hart converses like a man. The candelabra, statues, and chimney-pieces of Schloss Pommersfelden belong to the world of *Beauty and the Beast;* and the forests in Dürer engravings where knights meet Death and Cranach's Fountain of Youth where old women who bathe in it recover their beauty are instances of symbolic metamorphosis associated with natural forces. It is quite natural to find more collections of the wonders of nature in such countries than in sunny regions, and the galleries of Ambras and Hellbrunn, the pictures, the collections of antlers, of freak heads, and of furniture made from horns, and the cabinets filled with every variety of rock crystal, fossil, and coral, are simply aspects of pantheism. At the center of every grandiose Germanic dream one finds the cult of nature. The forests of Prussia, Austria, and Bavaria are extensions of the forests of Siberia. The Teutonic animist cult is a distant relative of Siberian Shamanism, and the Slavonic god in the Grotto of Neptune at Hellbrunn, with long-tongued mask, starting eyes, and bat's ears, is akin to the god of the forests found from the Eastern Siberia to the Alps. It is quite natural for a single vast expanse of forest to have preserved the same sylvan myths and legends up to the sixteenth century. One progresses imperceptibly from the steppes of Central Asia to the wooded tracts of Siberia and Germany, and the legends of nomads find their ultimate reflection in German palaces,

14

while those of the Latin world mirror only the Greco-Latin tradition.

There are no real dream palaces in France, Spain, Portugal, or Italy. Versailles and the Escorial are undoubtedly follies, but follies inspired by delusions of grandeur, rather than dreams. There was certainly nothing dreamlike about the Château de Versailles, built with the single intention of compelling the admiration of the nobility, summoned by royal command to entertainments, their enforced presence at court relieving the king of their potentially hostile absence on provincial estates. The vanished false pavilions and spectacular diversions of the Sun King were never more than a diplomatic and ingenious method of winning battles without fighting and of having fewer royal battalions to maintain. Versailles, which may well have been a folly, but a wise one, was the source of France's unity.

Kings and emperors have paid for their follies with their lives or the loss of their empires. Louis XIV's castle was the most profitable. Neither the wars of religion nor the Fronde achieved what a few fireworks, trellised arbors, and fountains succeeded in doing at Versailles. In France, wonders (in the sense implied here) are weapons or fashions, and French follies a means of imposing power.

The shellwork pavilion of Rambouillet, the vanished follies of the park of Chantilly, the grottoes of Thetis at Versailles, the Trianons, the Dairy of Rambouillet, the Hamlet of Versailles are merely the expression of a fashion (the word "folly" in the eighteenth century meant a house in a setting of "foliage"). One regarded a dream, or a dream decor, like spices or chocolates on one's table. One went to the grotto, the grove, or the maze for tea or casual amusement, not to indulge one's dreams. One played at shepherdesses and shepherds at the Hamlet of Versailles, and in the evening one returned to the Château; one drank milk at the dairy, and Marie Antoinette perhaps had her bosom molded to provide the pattern for a set of porcelain cups; but all this was just a manner of killing a few hours.

The "Desert" of Retz of M. de Monville, like the Bird's Dream of Rainer von Diez today, are quite exceptional in France. Yet the false pavilions of Retz were due, it seems, to Étienne Louis Boullée, one of the great visionary architects of the eighteenth century. And the Bird's Dream, the conception of a contemporary German theatrical producer, is the work of the sculptor of the extraordinary female figures called *Nanas*, Niki de Saint-Phalle.

In Latin countries, there has been little place for the marvelous in architecture. The Inquisition, mysticism, the conquest of America for Spain, and the occupation of Brazil by Portugal have not been factors favorable to its development. Italy alone turned away from the Latin world in this regard. The Renaissance, by officially adopting the cult of the man of Antiquity, concealed its antihumanism, reacting in favor of dreams and visionary perception. Rejecting logic and the classical proportions of the human body, it cultivated optical distortions, of which Michelangelo in the Sistine Chapel was the master.

This infatuation for *trompe-l'œil* and optical illusion immediately became a movement. Mannerism was initially only something "in the manner" of but as it grew in scope, it became a school which degenerated quickly. Nevertheless, it had time to produce a few curious masterpieces. Examples in literature are Ariosto's *Orlando Furioso* and his poems, which influenced Prince Orsini who ordered stone monsters for the Sacred Wood of Bomarzo surrounding his palace near Viterbo, Italy. As with the Ancients, mannerism offered liberty through dreams and dreamed visions and accepted all the adulteration provoked by it. In Italy liberty was in the rule and the rule in delirium.

The movement, however, was too brief and special to generate many masterpieces; Bomarzo was one of the few examples architecturally and sculpturally.

America also had its follies, which are among the strangest and most recent. Hearst's house at San Simeon represents a multimillionaire's dream of an earthly paradise, and one particularly close to us in time.

Place, race, climate, and religion seem to be the formative elements determining the quality of wonder in a palace, but they do not explain everything. Time also projects its dimensions over the dream, which is essentially the reflection of an epoch, that is to say of a particular society or personality.

Dreams of mass society exist as well as the dreams of individual dreamers. The curio rooms, the shellwork nymphaea, and the grottoes of the sixteenth century, the exotic Chinese and Indian pavilions of the eighteenth century, and the false ruins of the nineteenth century are typical examples of fashions. The dream was only a décor in which to dazzle. These palaces generally belonged to sociable individuals, who liked to entertain and to impress in order to please. The Swedish chinoiseries of Drottningholm, the mirrored drawing rooms and grottoes of the Margravine of Bayreuth, the follies of the parks at Nymphenburg and Schwetzingen, the shell-lined pavilion of Rambouillet, the Hamlet of Versailles, and the mock-Oriental décor of the Prince Regent at Brighton were all the product of fashion.

Enchanted Visions

Contrary to these altruistic dream palaces, designed for entertainment and pleasure, the palaces created because of a single dream appear as palaces of challenge and reflect, above all, one man and only incidentally a period—an eccentric, often misanthropic, sometimes genial, and always narcissistic man. These creations have no counterpart. The projection of one being and one life, they are unique.

Palaces of reveries are like theater stage sets waiting to welcome the public. Palaces of dreams have a public of only one, the dreamer himself. Ludwig II had operas performed in his private theater for him alone, and his castles were occupied only by servants. His palaces were sanctuaries, where the dream was worshiped as a god; the owner was the sole high priest, and contact with reality soon became impossible. Authoritarianism and madness stood at the palace gates. By the end of the reign of Ludwig II the only companions he had at Linderhof, Neuschwanstein, and Herrenchiemsee were his coachmen and valets, and his only guests the ghosts of Louis XVI and Marie Antoinette.

At Fonthill, Beckford dismissed from his mind everything which was not a part of his dream. A dwarf, a French monk, a cook, and two duennas served as his court—a galaxy weird enough to frighten the peasants who, when the octogenarian Beckford galloped through the countryside, took him for the devil. But not one of these faces woke the alert dreamer any more than the courtiers at the Villa Palagonia dared stir the hunchback prince who was its owner. The Prince of Palagonia dreamed of monsters; and his palace was inhabited by statues of the deformed, dwarfs, and clothed giraffes; and the ceilings of his drawing rooms were made of mirrors multiplying and distorting the reflections of his guests; his candelabra were formed of cracked tea-pots; and his chairs were studded with spikes to frustrate those tempted to sit down. The rules of this world, the inverse of the beautiful, were systematically applied to sculpture, architecture, decoration, and etiquette.

These singular dreams come from afar and all stem from a rich, sad, and lonely childhood. It is curious that *Orlando Furioso* was one of the favorite pieces of literature of Beckford in eighteenth-century England and of Ludwig II of Bavaria and his cousin Elizabeth of Austria nearly a hundred years later, as if this world of horror and violence were a necessity for them, and its excess the ruling passion of their lives.

The Sicilian prince at Palagonia, William Beckford at Fonthill, and Ludwig II of Bavaria in his castles went to the extreme end of the absolutes experienced in their childhood, but neither Ludwig's castles, overloaded with treasures, nor the masterpieces brought back from the continent by Beckford to Fonthill, succeeded in satisfying them. Their absolute quest for beauty and solitude through their "aesthetic phantoms" was only a search for the absolute in love, and their curious and unreal palaces only a step toward that reality.

"Life would not be possible
but for aesthetic phantoms."
—Nietzsche

The Hermitage of
the Margravine of Bayreuth

In a palace with quartz columns, a golden crown illuminated by candles rises into the air on a stream of water.

Bayreuth lies some fifty miles from Nuremberg. In the eighteenth century, the Bayreuth region became accustomed to unusual events during the construction of the Hermitage for the Margravine Wilhelmina, a sister of Frederick the Great.

Born in Berlin on July 3, 1709, daughter of the Elector of Brandenburg who became Frederick William I, King of Prussia, Wilhelmina married the son of the hereditary Margrave of Brandenburg-Bayreuth after a sad and sickly childhood.

Her French education, her interest and disposition for the arts, and her cult of friendship —like her brother Frederick II, she corresponded with Voltaire—soon singled her out in the luxurious atmosphere of the German courts at that time. A painter, she replaced the dismal official portraits on the walls of her palaces with the laughing faces of her friends and ladies-in-waiting. The music room in the Hermitage "is decorated with fine white marble and the compartments are green," wrote the Margravine in her *Memoirs*. "In each compartment is a well-made music trophy; portraits of several fine-looking people by the most skillful painters have been hung above the trophies and set in the wall in gilded frames; the background of the ceiling is white; relief work represents Orpheus playing a lyre and charming animals; all of the relief work is gilded; my harpsichord and all the music instruments have been placed in this room at one end of which is my study. This room is varnished brown and contains miniature paintings of natural flowers; this is where I am writing these memoirs and where I spend many hours thinking." A few miles from Bayreuth, the castle is located in a romantic park dotted with follies, pavilions, fountains, and statues.

The Margravine also had an abbey built near the castle, but its porous rock exterior, creating a gloomy structure reminiscent of dismal Anglican chapels in poor regions of Great Britain, in no way suggests its ornate interior. Seeking contrast by lining the most dismal of exteriors with elaborate decoration shows a lack of naturalness; but no one can speak of naturalness at the Hermitage, where everything is artificial and designed to surprise. The theater built in 1743 is a false ruin, and the performances took place in the garden.

The abbey opens on an inner courtyard off which were the Margravine's apartments built around a cool chamber under the belfry of the chapel.

Germany

Because of her education and fondness for everything French, Wilhelmina readily accepted the vogue for the rococo style which had then conquered a large part of Europe although she gave it a distinctive mark by substituting elements borrowed from nature for purely abstract decorative motifs. A number of small drawing rooms come next including music rooms decorated with gilded violins, flutes, and lyres. Their walls are adorned with a host of grotesque figures, monkeys, butterflies, Chinamen and flowers. Other drawing rooms lead to the curious mirror room—a small drawing room with yellow eighteenth-century wood paneling set off by blue. The moldings of the wood paneling are inlaid with countless fragments of mirrors, the shapes of which are like those found in Ming summer palaces of China— diamond-shaped forms, round spots and glass designs which interreflect. China is more Chinese in the Hermitage than it ever was in the Celestial Empire.

An almost similar small drawing room was built for the Margravine at the castle of La Favorite near Baden-Baden where the Margravine enjoyed masquerades. Grand ladies of the eighteenth century evidently loved the unusual setting of paneled walls and mirrors, where a single sofa faced a few chairs, a drawing room planned for the effect of surprise contrived by mirrors which produced fragmented reflections of their guests.

If a residence has one or two dazzling rooms, its other features may be overlooked. The grotto tends to dominate one's impression of the Hermitage. It is reached by a few steps and consists of a square room entirely covered with small pebbles and decorated with porous rock arches and shellwork. Wilhelmina's initials in red and white pebbles are crowned by the heads of monsters with oyster mouths and hair made of shells. Sirens and dolphins in mother-of-pearl and stucco frolic in the angles above the recesses between the columns decorated with reliefs made of stucco.

In the center of the room stands a small rock on which is the golden crown of the Margravine, illuminated, like a chandelier, with candles, the flame of which replaces the brilliance of precious stones. A stream of water rising suddenly from the rock lifts the glittering crown ten feet into the air where it hovers between heaven and earth. A number of other jets form a circle around the rock and add to the theatrical magic of the scene. The crown eventually sinks gently to the ground on a diminishing stream of water until it comes to rest on the rock.

Another glittering spectacle is seen in the great central pool with many fountains in front of the colonnaded residence: columns of rock crystal, walls of lapis lazuli, white and red marble, silver busts, and fountains to reflect them, and statues representing scenes of abduc-

The Hermitage of the Margravine of Bayreuth

tion that were planned to surprise guests. This site becomes a dazzling theater set when the sun strikes the thousand rock crystals and the faces of bronze emperors and turns the crystal columns into prisms which reflect the sun's rays as spots of color onto the marble floors.

Almost everywhere in the park pavilions have been built in the middle of groves, in arbors along the edges of lawns and woods, and at a bridge in front of the large Fountain of Nymphs, in which innumerable jets play.

The Hermitage of the Margravine Wilhelmina was used as a meeting place by King Ludwig II of Bavaria and the composer Richard Wagner after a long separation. Wagner had gone there alone on April 17, 1871. Arriving at Bayreuth, he hurried to the Hermitage, where the caretaker led him from room to room. He then went into the garden and, discovering an apparently splendid site on an adjoining property, decided that his future home should be located there and that a theater in which his operas would be performed should be built on the heights above the town.

Friends and lovers of his music would come from all parts of the world to hear it. At fifty-eight he had more confidence and hope than at twenty; moreover, Ludwig II would surely support him in his project. The theater was a folly, but Ludwig was used to building mad castles and consequently understood him better than anyone. However, the king wrote

in that same month of April, 1871: "I don't like Wagner's plan very much. Performing the complete *Ring* at Bayreuth next year is clearly impossible. I want this understood in writing." He was to regret this letter, and later subscribed 75,000 marks for the project. In the spring of 1872 "the Bayreuth era of civilization" began. Although the king was not present, the first stone of the theater was laid. Ludwig was again invited to contribute, but he was said to have been annoyed with the composer for "personal and secret reasons."

The truth was that the king wanted Wagner to compose the music for a Latin hymn *Macte Imperator* by one of his protégés, Felix Dahn, while Wagner was finishing *Götterdämmerung*.

Wagner was still appealing for help from the king when Ludwig replied to him: "No, no, and again no. It must not end this way. We shall have to help you." And he opened a credit of 300,000 marks for Wagner's Festspielhaus.

By the end of July, 1876, Bayreuth was ready for the festival. At 1 A.M. on August 6 a special train stopped in an open field. A tall man emerged from the train; Ludwig II had come secretly to meet Wagner. They greeted each other without a word and left together in a carriage. They had not met for eight years. The carriage drove Ludwig and Wagner to the Hermitage. That night, the

Germany

Margravine's eccentric drawing rooms, planned for frivolity, enclosed two remarkable men whose friendship had cooled, and silently watched the resurrection, for one night at least, of the greatest passion in Ludwig's reign.

We know nothing of what was said between the two that night. They may have tried to discuss the reasons for the sadness from which Ludwig II had not recovered. Building castles does not efface the memory of wounded friendship. When the king and the composer parted at dawn, they left each other after spending the night with their memories as one spends a night with a dead body; as dawn broke, only solitude was left to each—madness for Ludwig and glory for Wagner.

The next day Ludwig attended the rehearsal of *Das Rheingold*, the prologue to Wagner's opera trilogy. At 7 P.M., the king, taking a short cut, walked to the Festspielhaus; he disliked crowds too much to appear officially and secretly entered a box where Wagner was waiting for him. It was the last dress rehearsal; and the king was so delighted that he agreed to return to the Hermitage that night in a closed carriage and even to drive through the town. The day after, the public was allowed to attend the rehearsal of *Die Walküre*. An hour after the curtain fell, the king disappeared and returned to his special train in the open country for the trip back to the mountains.

On the night of August 26-27, 1876, Ludwig's train again stopped in the fields near Bayreuth. The king emerged incognito to attend the last performance of *The Ring*. He was recognized in his box and was applauded all the way from the Hermitage to his train. The Hermitage was never again to see Wagner and Ludwig II together. It had been the setting of their final hope. Was it deceived? This remains a secret: neither ever spoke about it. After that, Ludwig thought only of his castle of Herrenchiemsee, which he had begun to build. In 1883, when the funeral train carrying Wagner's body stopped in Munich for a last public tribute to the composer, the king was not there, probably because of his dislike for crowds. He may, however, have preferred to remember the night of August 5-6, 1876, in the drawing rooms of the Margravine Wilhelmina.

1. *The Margravine Wilhelmina of Bayreuth, a close friend of Voltaire, built the Hermitage, the fantastic character of which is caught in this fountain view.*

2

3

2. *The central pavilion of the Hermitage.*

3. *Entrance hall leading to the salons of the Hermitage. Above the fireplace, a portrait of the Margrave of Bayreuth.*

4. *The closet of mirrors.*

5. *Seen from the exterior, the Hermitage looks like a chapel.*

6. *The Margravine's grotto.*

7. *The Margravine's crown lighted by candles. A stream of water can lift up the crown and suspend it in air without extinguishing the candles.*

4

5

6

7

◁ 8. *Columns made of quartz; walls of lapis lazuli and marble; silver-plated busts. Unusual materials for a mannerist palace.*

9. *The dome of the grotto.* ▷

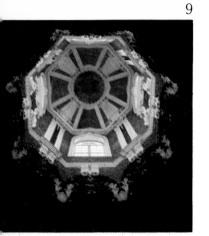

9

10

△

. *The salon in which Ludwig II
et Wagner.*

. *Sea horse and child.*

. *The doors of the grotto with the* ▷
*itials of Wilhelmina beneath shell-
ork.*

12

14

15

◁ 13. *A pavilion beside a pond in the Hermitage park.*

◁ 14-15. *Two statues in front of the main fountain depict scenes of abduction.*

16. *A false Chinese pavilion.*

The Castles of King Ludwig II of Bavaria

Linderhof, a castle, a theater, a grotto, a bedroom, and a piano for Wagner who never came.

"An eternal enigma, that is what I want to be to myself and to others," wrote King Ludwig II of Bavaria in one of his letters; and he applied himself to the task of being quixotic. Even if he had not wished it, the blood of his family, the Wittelsbachs, would have made him enigmatic. Ludwig II had a dreamy, passionate, and idealistic character. He became misanthropic only after the deception of his early loves and enthusiasm. His interests then turned to building, through which he expected to realize the dreams of beauty which Wagner, politics—"nonsense of government"—and his friendship with artists and peasants could not effectively satisfy.

Ludwig's ultimate enthusiasm was for castles, and in the mid-nineteenth century he wished to create them on a scale equal to those built in the Middle Ages or the reign of Louis XIV. The drama which he acted before the eyes of his subjects and the world was to last fifteen years, long enough for him to build three great structures. The curtain fell for Ludwig and he was arrested for delusions of grandeur just as he was planning a fourth palace.

Today, the beauty of these castles no longer impresses, although the splendor of the sites and the extravagant architectural plagiarism astonish us. Linderhof evokes the Trianon, but is snowbound six months every year. Neuschwanstein is a copy of a medieval Rhineland castle; and, in its rustic solitude, Herrenchiemsee is a replica of Versailles complete with the Hall of Mirrors, the King's State Bedroom, and the Ambassadors' Staircase.

The presence of Ludwig, and Ludwig alone, is everywhere in these castles, through his attempt to revive the past. His household gods were not his own ancestors, but rather the homes of the characters whom he would have wished to be. In the end, he was called to account as much for his unpractical romanticism as his extravagance. However, his castles, opened to the public a few months after his death, have always provided the state with revenue. The object is not important as long as there is love; but the object of Ludwig's passion, whether Wagner or castles, was always in conflict with his time. For him power derived from divine right. At the dawn of the mechanical age, he was still intellectually and hereditarily immersed in the noble traditions of the great reigning families and could not disavow his role as an absolute king acting in accordance with his own pleasure. As a young man

33

17. *Ludwig II, with his mother and his brother Otto, feeding swans. Ludwig's taste for the fantastic was acquired early in life. The castles he built, with immense parks, incarnated his childhood dreams.*

Germany

Ludwig was a dreamer; as a king, he still dreamed and exploited his position to realize his dreams.

Born in 1845 at the Nymphenburg, the palace of a thousand follies near Munich, the future Ludwig II was a handsome child who lived in a world of legends. His Prussian mother collected everything dealing with swans for the Schloss (Castle) Berg, but her tenderness for this bird did not extend to her son, who remembered only his mother's severity. She is depicted, nonetheless, scattering bread to the swans with her two children, Ludwig and Otto. In fact, Ludwig was always left alone. His tutors, who used to see him spend many hours without playing, deplored the wasted time and wondered why "Your Highness does not get something to read, instead of growing bored with nothing to do?" But Ludwig would reply: "Oh! I am not at all bored. I amuse myself by imagining beautiful things." He was allowed no friend of his own age; he was given no pocket money; and he would sometimes be whipped by his father, Maximilian. The first time he was given money as an adolescent, Ludwig hurried to a jeweler's window in Munich and wanted to buy everything.

As a thirteen-year-old boy, Ludwig secretly sight-read Wagner's *Lohengrin* and learned it by heart. In 1861, *Tannhäuser* and *Lohengrin* were performed at the Munich Opera. Ludwig, at his own request, had been allowed to attend.

At the sound of the music, he became entranced. "When Tannhäuser returned to the Venusberg," wrote his attendant, "the prince's body was convulsed with spasms so violent that I feared an attack of epilepsy." All of Ludwig's extreme sensitivity had been exposed, and from that moment he had only one aim: to hear, see, meet, and help Wagner. When their friendship crumbled, Ludwig returned to his wild mountain rides and thought only of plans for his castles, which had already been started during his friendship with Wagner.

In 1864, the composer dominated the affections of the young eighteen-year-old king. Wagner told a friend in Zürich at that time: "You can have no idea of the magic in his expression. But he is, alas, so handsome and so full of intelligence that I am afraid of seeing his life vanish like a divine dream in this ignoble world." "I believe," he wrote, "that if he were to die, I too would die an instant later."

Ludwig II was possessed by a passion. His friendship was like love. Through the king, the composer went to live in Bavaria with Hans von Bülow, the famous conductor, and his wife Cosima, Liszt's daughter. Wagner wrote of his patron: "He is insatiable for science and love; and his insatiability does not belong in this world." To please Ludwig, Wagner dressed in silk and velvet clothes, wore berets and fur capes. In Munich, Wagner was suspected of intrigue, and Ludwig reminded people of his grandfather because of his sudden and extreme infatuation. Ludwig I, people said, had his Lola and Ludwig II has his "Lolus." They were referring to the infatuation of Ludwig's grandfather, Ludwig I, for Lola Montez. The press did everything possible to separate the king from Wagner. "His Majesty must choose between the love and happiness of his people and the friendship of a man despised by every good and wholesome element in the kingdom." Reluctantly Ludwig sent Wagner abroad. When the king was imprisoned for having no other thought than the construction of his castles, the fact that everything he had ever loved had been taken away from him was forgotten. Not until later was he credited, along with Nietzsche, for being one of the first to recognize Wagner's genius.

After his separation from Wagner, Ludwig took refuge on his island, the Roseninsel in Lake Starnberg near Munich. His castle was surrounded by 15,000 rose bushes. His only friend at this time was his cousin, Elizabeth, Empress of Austria, with whom he had much in common. Together they would read Ariosto, who seems to have been a favorite author of eccentric people of the period. When Ludwig wrote to his cousin, he would sign himself "the eagle to the dove." The Empress once said of him: "He lived only for his dreams, and his sadness was dearer to him than all life itself."

On the Roseninsel both loved to cultivate this sadness, and there Ludwig might well have declaimed Hamlet's soliloquy, for in his enigmatic traits he was the very embodiment of the Prince of Denmark:

For who would bear the whips and scorns of time,
The oppressor's wrong, the proud man's contumely,
The pangs of despised love,
The insolence of office,
When he himself might his quietus make
With a bare bodkin?

The Prince von Hohenlohe was concerned about Ludwig's attitude. "Nobody any longer saw the king, who was living with the Prince von Thurn und Taxis when he was not with his groom Völk on the Roseninsel where they amused themselves with fireworks." This was the moment in 1866 chosen by the Prussians to attack Bavaria, which was defeated at Dornbach and Kissingen. A month later peace came in exchange for three Franconian cantons. Bismarck exacted 30,000,000 marks. Ludwig refused to see his mother because she was a Prussian princess.

In January, 1867, Ludwig proposed marriage to Sophie, the younger sister of Elizabeth of Austria. He postponed the ceremony for months and, on October 10, 1867, broke off the engagement causing a great court scandal. The strain of his friendship with Wagner,

Germany

Bavaria's defeat by Prussia, and his broken engagement may help to explain Ludwig's follies.

The king occasionally slipped away from Bavaria. He went to Paris in July, 1867, under the pretext of visiting the Paris Exhibition. Napoleon III had taken him to the château of Pierrefonds, where he had been intoxicated by the spirit of Joan of Arc, and to Versailles, where the aura of Louis XIV inspired in him the desire to create a Versailles of his own in Bavaria. While in Paris, Ludwig bought a Moorish pavilion, which he sent to Linderhof.

Wagner, Sophie, and affairs of state were now forgotten. Only Ludwig II remained to face Louis XIV and Ludwig himself. The result was his fantastic structures, a substitute for the unattainable glory of power, a fulfillment of dreams, and the climax of a yearning for solitude.

The king understood the position of a Bavaria subordinate to the aggressive Prussia; and his romantic follies and despair, until now dormant, and the profound tendencies of which they were a reflection, were intensified by the situation of his country. The hereditary disease of the Wittelsbach line affected him, but it was Otto, more than he, who had been really tainted, barking at the windows of the Nymphenburg palace under the delusion that he was a dog. It was easy to claim that, although Ludwig did not bark at windows, he, never-

theless, threw the country's resources out of them to build his castles.

Linderhof is located in the Graswang valley near the village of Garmisch-Partenkirchen. A small hunting lodge which Ludwig visited as a youth stood there, and Linderhof is an extension of that humble building. The reconstruction was begun in 1870, and the architect Georg von Dollman pressed on with the job, for Ludwig wanted to occupy his palace as quickly as possible. Work was essentially finished in 1879 and the only major change made after completion of the castle was the enlargement of the king's bedroom in 1884, two years before Ludwig's death.

The park of Linderhof, designed by Karl von Effner, owes much of its charm to the ingenuity with which he used the natural contours of the site to integrate the French rococo castle into the harsh grandeur of the mountain landscape. The gardens, filled with sculpture, were completed in 1880.

The king filled the park and woods stretching to the south of the house with various buildings. In addition to the Moorish pavilion from Paris, these included structures inspired by Wagner's operas. Of these only the Grotto of Venus survives. Two, one inspired by the forest decor of *Die Walküre* and the other by Gurnemanz's hut in the third act of *Parsifal*, were destroyed by fire and pillaging in 1945. Plans, sketches, and models

36

for other buildings conceived for the Linderhof park remain, but they were not realized in any other way.

When the castle of Linderhof, a quadrangular building of imitation freestone with a second elegant story decorated with statues, emerged, it seemed to have everything: a salon with Gobelins tapestries, an elaborate rose boudoir, a lilac salon, a cabinet room, a lapis lazuli study, ivories, blue fireplaces made of marble from the Urals, rosewood furniture, Dresden china, malachite suites. A bust of Marie Antoinette was one of the adornments in the garden. From the windows of the palace walks could be seen, extending under arches of greenery.

Although intended as a kind of Trianon, Linderhof externally resembles the summer-houses imagined by Russian princes, half-hidden behind fountains amid statues and flower beds. Louis XV and Louis XVI are the dominant styles of the furnishings—mauve and pink settees and chairs, lapis lazuli fireplaces, innumerable tables on delicate hand-woven carpets, mirrors reflecting the silver drapes and curtains, whose extravagant tassels and trimmings are Victorian in style, not Louis XV. These sharp contrasts in décor provide the charm of Linderhof. The state apartments furnished with bronze objects and skins edged with blue silk under tables made of blue Dresden inlay create a dazzling baroque setting.

The taste of South Central Europe, whether Austrian or Bavarian, borrowed from eighteenth-century France the proportions of its salons and its use of paneling, from Russia malachite, from Bohemia crystal and glass, from Italy little Pompeian tables of the period of Paulina Borghese, and from Saxony furniture. Thus, a mixture of styles was featured at Linderhof, all choices being determined by the king, who would have liked to spend his life with Louis XIV or Louis XV, and in lieu of that found solace with the stags and wild boars of his forests. Ludwig called his castle Meicost-Ettal, an anagram of *L'Etat, c'est moi.* He had his bed placed at the center of the park and of the palace, under a cobalt-blue velvet canopy surrounded by golden cupids. When he rose, before his feet touched the marble floor, they would rest on the skins of animals which he and his men had hunted in his forests.

Ludwig chose to use Linderhof as a place of solitude. He always dined alone, raising the ready-laid table from the basement by means of a trap-door opening in the floor—an eighteenth-century tradition. He sometimes sat with two vacant places at his table reserved for the ghosts of Marie Antoinette and Louis XVI, the only guests, he would say, who went away when one wished them to.

Receiving ministers or nobility was distasteful to the king. When he could not avoid it, he had a huge bouquet of flowers placed in the

Germany

center of the table to hide his visitor. Such incidents could not be forgotten and, when multiplied, made Ludwig's capacity for kingship suspect. Dispatches were delivered at Linderhof by ministers, who came from Munich by carriage. If the king was out hunting, he was notified. A table would be set up in a field, and while huntsmen, hounds, and grooms waited, Ludwig would talk hurriedly, decide, sign, remount, and vanish into the forests in front of his offended ministers.

The music room was a typical caprice. Everything was arranged for Wagner's arrival but the composer never went to Linderhof, and the piano, encased in priceless woods and guarded by a Sèvres peacock, remained unused. In the main entrance of the castle is an equestrian statue of Louis XIV and, on the king's desk, a portrait of Louis XV. There are no pictures of Ludwig himself, but mirrors were everywhere. The throne room is small, but its ermine dais immense.

The theater in the park, an auditorium for ten people, is a curious artificial grotto closed by a massive stone, which moves on iron hinges and opens onto a subterranean lake, reflecting a tiny stage. The lake serves as the orchestra pit. There is no place for the public. In an angle to one side is the royal box. One sees simply a boat with two seats, a painted shell adorned with cupids, around which white swans once glided in the darkness. The boat

was to carry the king and Wagner, as they listened to the composer's music. The king amused himself with performances given for himself alone, or for a few grooms or opera singers, the former brought from his estates, the latter from Munich. A particular friend for a time about 1881 was the actor Joseph Kainz. A guest enjoyed the right to the furs of the royal box, which blazed with an inferno of red and green lights concealed in the stucco stalactites of the ceiling.

The grotto is not the only strange room at Linderhof. In the park the Moorish pavilion that the king bought at the Paris Exhibition rises above a garden. Ludwig had it converted into a throne room—an Arabian fountain and a huge ottoman made of pink and gold brocaded silk surmounted by bronze peacocks, the fan of their tail feathers decorated with "eyes" of precious stones. Linderhof is an ode to narcissism. The birds are symbolic, a substitute for the swans of Schloss Berg.

The king in his solitude became more eccentric. He signed himself in Spanish "*Yo el Rey*" ("I the King"). At night a sleigh covered with bells and embroidered ermine rugs would be harnessed at his request. A few grooms would go out with him. The king was stealing silently away by torchlight. The sound of his voice could be heard above the jingle of the sleigh bells, reciting poetry. A man on horseback preceded the sleigh, probably his groom

Hornig, to whom the king was devoted, or some other young man from the country. Ludwig inspired true devotion, and of course none refused to saddle his mount, despite the cold or the time of night. These were the men who understood him perhaps because he really loved them. When he was reproached for liking people not of his position, he would say that he preferred the conversation of those "who see no further than their bottles." This annoyed the nobility. A king, whose advisers were peasants, who recited poetry alone at night, who rode about night and day escorted by his valets disguised as French footmen wearing wigs, cocked hats, and eighteenth-century Versailles livery, could not be taken seriously. A painting commissioned by Ludwig, slightly demented in conception, shows him flitting through the moonlight with his retinue.

In 1869 the king began his private diary:

"Report: (an outline of the life of the great King) 8 o'clock: moonlight. Race with Reutte [acrobatic rider] at Plansee. The lovely sleighs, in magic moonlight, [gliding] through forests of fir-trees covered with snow. At midnight back to dear Linderhof the glory of Meicost-Ettal...

"By order of the King.

"Banished forever from the heaven of the royal bed to the two cushions of an ottoman... However, here, never anymore; in any event not before February 10. And then ever more infrequently, ever more infrequently... Here there is none of your 'for such is our good pleasure.' It is an absolute law.

> *Toute justice émane du Roy*
> *Si veut le Roy, veut la loi.*
> *Une foi, une loi, un Roy.*

"By order of the King.
                    Ludwig."

The king continued his moonlight escapades while Bismarck tried to persuade him to join Prussia in attacking Napoleon III of France. He accepted the alliance, and his troops were among those that defeated Napoleon III at Sedan. Ludwig felt no glory from this—on the contrary. Invited to the victory festivities in Munich, he replied: "Do you think it's fun to be devoured?" He refused to participate.

Was it madness or sanity to show no pleasure in this event? Ludwig believed that because of the dominance of Prussia the celebrations in no way enhanced the glory of the Wittelsbachs. It was madness to remain at Linderhof thought his ministers. The German Confederation was a reality. Bavaria could never be Queen of a Southern Germany opposed to Prussia. On July 16, 1871, Ludwig murmured, as he mounted his horse: "This is my first ride as a vassal." It was his sole reaction to

Germany

the victory at Sedan. "He is mad." This was the general consensus. The King of Prussia, Ludwig's cousin, was surprised by his absence from the festivities in Munich. Ludwig, although he agreed to do and sign whatever he must, faced the situation with passive resistance. He would attend no celebration. Performances, if such there must be, would be for him alone, hidden in his curtain-shrouded box.

Ludwig's conduct became increasingly peculiar. Trifles enraged him. When one of his servants behaved stupidly, he put a wax seal on the man's forehead, which he had to wear when on duty to show that his mind was completely blocked. Another servant who appeared unsatisfactory was threatened with a revolver. Still another, who made a mistake, was crushed between two doors.

The king moved constantly from one castle to another. He liked to survey the world from a window, alone, knowing that the building was empty. It is impossible to live, Nietzsche wrote, except in art, and life is only possible with the help of aesthetic phantoms. Ludwig dreamed of these phantoms which he conjured up on his nocturnal ramblings.

18

18. *Linderhof was built between 1870 and 1879. Ludwig was inspired by the Grand Trianon at Versailles, but* *Linderhof is too exuberantly German baroque to be a copy of that neoclassic building.*

19. *The artificial grotto and subterranean lake at Linderhof, where Wagnerian operas were performed for Ludwig's single pleasure while he drifted in a boat surrounded by swans.*

19

21

21. *The three Rhine maidens being moved by stage hands in an early performance of* Das Rheingold.

◁ 20. *A satirical drawing of Ludwig in Wagner's shadow.*

23. *Ludwig's gilt carriage: an eighteenth century folly in the nineteenth century.* ▷

22. *One of Ludwig's many sleighs, now displayed in the castle of Nymphenburg.*
▽

20

22

24

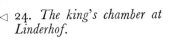

◁ 24. *The king's chamber at Linderhof.*

25. *One of the state apart-* ▷
ments at Linderhof.

25

Next pages:
28. *A sleigh ride in below-freezing temperature through the Linderhof mountains.*

26. *The Moorish pavilion at Linderhof, which Ludwig bought in Paris at the 1867 Exposition.*

27. *The throne of a king who loved only solitude was* ▷
decorated with glass peacocks made to order in Munich.

26

The Castles of
King Ludwig II of Bavaria

(Continued)

Neuschwanstein, an eagle's nest, and Herrenchiemsee, a copy of Versailles, the last two follies of Ludwig II, the mad king.

Ludwig based the plan of Neuschwanstein on the knightly strongholds of the Rhine, on the Gothic style in general, and on the thirteenth-century fortress in particular. He was inspired by painting rather than by architecture. The family castle of Hohenschwangau, within binocular range of the new castle projected by Ludwig, had cradled his childhood. Linderhof is also nearby, some 15 miles from Neuschwanstein. Ludwig wanted a castle larger than that of his father, King Maximilian. Maximilian had a perforated canopy above his bed which enabled starlight to enter his room and which was regulated by buttons. The evening star could shine in the darkness above the king's bed, illuminating the frescoes of the walls on which the heroines of ancient legend played among swans. Perhaps this fancy shows a hint of the extravagance which Ludwig later was to exaggerate.

Ludwig did not conceive of Neuschwanstein as a place in which to live comfortably. He wanted to realize the concept of a castle in its essence, with turrets, watch towers, drawbridges, interior courtyards, and ramparts on a precipice at the top of a peak. The castle has a guard room on the ground floor as well as suites and state apartments on the third and fourth floors, which were not finished until after Ludwig's death. The corridors, staircases, and windows are carved with thirteenth-century decorations, and the paintings and frescoes on the walls depict old legends, that of Sigurd (called Siegfried in the Nibelungen) and of Gudrun, two characters from the Old Norse Edda.

The suites are done in the pseudo-medieval syle of the "Burgen" built in the nineteenth century along the banks of the Rhine. The throne room is Byzantine in concept. Ludwig commissioned a painting of himself as he would have looked in this room at his coronation, but the coronation did not take place and the room was never used. The throne room leads to the king's apartment—a blue waiting room; duty-officer's room; study with a combined desk and cabinet, oak chair, opaline lamps, faience stove painted with the legend of Tannhäuser, and green silk curtains embroidered in gold. Leading to the king's chamber is a corridor transformed into a grotto of stalactites with colored lighting. It recalls the cave of Hörselberg in the legend of Tannhäuser.

The king believed that the Lohengrin legend was connected with Neuschwanstein (New Rock of the Swan), for Lohengrin first appeared in a boat drawn by swans. Symbols

29. *An angel about to crown Ludwig II suggests that he build new castles.*

of swans are repeated on the doors, in the coats of arms, and on the porcelain, and a huge swan in white majolica rests on a massive ornamental flower-stand. On the wall of the large drawing room Lohengrin is shown facing Telramund and greeting Elsa; Elsa is depicted questioning Lohengrin although she had sworn before marrying him never to question him about his origin. Tristan and Isolde and the Ring of the Nibelungen are also illustrated. The waiting room has a ceiling like a pergola with majolica facings in Pompeian colors, opaline lamps, and a jewel box.

Ludwig's medieval bedroom has Gothic paneling and a central pillar carved of oak. The style is a mid-nineteenth century longing for the Middle Ages, reflecting the décor which was called Tudor in England and Troubadour in France and which reflected nostalgia in all European countries for the days of chivalry. The king's bed is the masterpiece of the castle, more typically Gothic in its delicately pierced carving than any of the other woodwork. It is an insomniac's bed, made for one who longed to dream and craved for sumptuous decoration, with curtains of blue brocade. It has been said that this special blue, found in the bedrooms of all Ludwig's castles, is a psychological symbol for a maternal fixation. It may have been the blue which he had admired at Versailles. Blue and white were also the heraldic colors of Bavaria, which was dedicated to the Virgin Mary.

The headboard seems to have been copied from the sketchbook of Viollet-le-Duc, the famous nineteenth-century restorer. It recalls a bit of the cathedrals of Amiens or Chartres. The washstand is a jumble of turrets and Gothic vaulting in the middle of which is a silver basin surmounted by a swan, through whose head and beak the water flows. Ludwig's Neuschwanstein bed is unique among his castle beds because two sides are against the walls. At Linderhof and Herrenchiemsee, the royal beds are in the middle of the room. Perhaps he considered Neuschwanstein an impregnable eagle's nest.

In the meantime, Ludwig built his last folly, Herrenchiemsee, the third castle of the trilogy, the new Versailles, which was to cost his life. Herrenchiemsee is on the island of Herreninsel on Chiemsee Lake, some 50 miles southeast of Munich. Ludwig grew more fantastically extravagant, and his ministers cut off his supply of money. Herrenchiemsee was only partly completed when the blow fell. Furious, Ludwig appealed to his cousin Frederick of Prussia. He had, in fact, a right to a share of the large sum paid by France after the defeat of 1870, but Bismarck refused. Ludwig turned to the House of Orléans without success, and then to the Rothschild Bank, which remained unsympathetic.

Nevertheless, much had been achieved at Herrenchiemsee. The king's bedroom, splendid in blue and gold, is 45 feet long, slightly longer than Louis XIV's at Versailles. The main façade of the castle, 340 feet wide, has twenty-three windows. The staircase is 115 feet long and 42 feet wide. The Hall of Mirrors, 250 feet long, is adorned with busts of Condé, Turenne, Vauban, Villars and allegorical statues of Peace, War, the Arts, and the Sciences. The furniture copied from Versailles includes a roll-top desk by Jean Henri Riesener, an astronomical clock and a medal cabinet never finished (the arms on the door are still missing). Everything irritated Ludwig, who spent only ten days a year every summer at the castle to verify the quality and authenticity of the contents. He dug his umbrella into groups of marble only to find that they were plaster, or pulled an orange off an orange tree in the Hall of Mirrors to discover that it was attached by wire.

This was the state of his unfinished copy of the Château of Versailles when his funds were cut off. He sent an emissary across the ocean to buy a new land where a king could be king. "And how do we pay?" asked Richard Hornig. Ludwig whispered into the ear of his coachman-chancellor the appalling reply: "By selling Bavaria." On his return, the emissary reported that he had not found the object of Ludwig's dreams. Bavaria was not sold, but the king was soon to be deposed.

Ministers in the Bavarian government voted that Ludwig be arrested on the grounds of insanity. What form of insanity? It was easy to obtain the reports of several psychiatrists who stated without examining the king that he was incapable of ruling. Prince Luitpold, Ludwig's uncle, was appointed regent.

A first commission went to Neuschwanstein, where Ludwig was living. A coachman at an inn overheard the plan and warned the king, who barricaded the castle. The whole village blocked the delegation, whom they threatened to throw into the dungeons. All were captured, except one who ran off to telegraph Munich. The government officially removed the king from office. At Neuschwanstein the commissioners were secretly freed once it was learned that Ludwig had been deposed. Two officials accompanied by doctors and orderlies reached the castle on Friday, June 11, 1886, and stated that they wanted to examine the king. Ludwig II demanded the key of the highest tower, intending to leap to his death. The key could not be found, but Ludwig was asked to come forward so that it could be handed to him. He did so and was promptly seized by concealed orderlies—a familiar ruse.

Ludwig II was transferred to the castle of Berg. He smiled at seeing his family home transformed into a guarded asylum. Barricades had been installed and every door had a peep-hole.

Ludwig seemed very calm... The next day was Pentecost. Doctor Bernhard von Gudden who was in attendance sent news to Munich that all was well. At five o'clock in the afternoon he went for a walk with the king. Ludwig did not want to be followed by the orderlies, so Gudden dismissed them. Subsequent events remain a mystery. That evening the drowned bodies of Ludwig and Gudden were found in the lake. The king's overcoat was floating at his side, and the doctor's face was scratched and his neck showed signs of strangulation.

The alarm had been given by the discovery of the king's hat and Gudden's umbrella on the bank. Had Ludwig tried to escape by swimming to the opposite bank, where Elizabeth of Austria, who was known to be in the neighborhood, may have been waiting for him? Did Gudden try to force him to return?

Did the king club the doctor with his field glasses, and with one man drowning, did the other drown himself, too? The mystery remains unsolved.

In the evening the body of Ludwig II lay in the chapel of the castle of Berg surrounded by flowers. Elizabeth went there immediately, and was the first to stand vigil.

Ludwig in death had gone to join Siegfried, Lohengrin, Parsifal, and other legendary heroes. He had sought inspiration for his life by building castles. He had wanted a life of isolation, but succeeded only in making himself legendary. Long after his death Bavarian peasants still tattooed their chests with the features of the mad king.

30. *Neuschwanstein Castle. Ludwig's eagle-nest overlooks a river, a few miles from the old family castle at Hohenschwangau.*

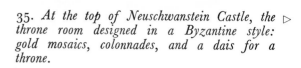

35. At the top of Neuschwanstein Castle, the throne room designed in a Byzantine style: gold mosaics, colonnades, and a dais for a throne.

◁ 31. Princess Sophie—the daughter of Maximilian, Duke of Bavaria, and sister of Elizabeth of Austria—with her fiancé Ludwig II.

32. The Byzantine throne room ▷ at Neuschwanstein. This painting depicts a coronation that never took place.

31

32

33. Ludwig and Joseph Kainz. The king discovered the actor in Munich and invited him to Linderhof. For a trip to Switzerland, he had passports made under the names of the Marquis de Saverny and Didier, two characters in Marion Delorme, a play by Victor Hugo in which Kainz played the role of Didier.

34. Kainz sitting, Ludwig standing. Their places are interchangeable, a proof of the king's friendship. But one night, when

Kainz was reciting poetry to the king on the edge of a lake, he suddenly became weary and asked permission to stop. Ludwig embarked and went away in a boat, leaving the actor alone. When Kainz arrived at their residence, the king had already packed and was ready to return to his castle. Later he sent Kainz a painting of the lake as a farewell present. Hurt, Kainz returned it. Ludwig sought in vain for an ideal relationship. When he became disappointed, he turned his back and tried to forget.

33

34

35

Next pages:

37. *Ludwig's childhood bedroom at Hohenschwangau.*

38-39. *The bedroom of Ludwig's father, Maximilian II, at Hohenschwangau.*

40. *A study in one of the towers at Hohenschwangau, from which Ludwig supervised the construction of Neuschwanstein Castle. Using binoculars, he was able to watch progress, issue instructions, and hasten the completion of the fantastic structure.*

41. *Ludwig's study in his new castle at Neuschwanstein.*

42. *Ludwig's bedroom with silver swan, washbasin, and murals on the walls.*

36. *A corridor at Neuschwanstein transformed into a stalactite grotto leads to the king's bedroom.*

36

37

38

39

40

41

43. *Ludwig II in 1864.* 43

44. *Ludwig II in 1874.* 44

45. *Ludwig II in 1886.* 45

46

47

46. *Ludwig II lying in state in the castle at Berg. He was found drowned in a lake with the doctor who had been attending him.*

◁ 47. *A copy of the Louis XIV staircase from Versailles at Herrenchiemsee. The original in the French palace was destroyed in the eighteenth century, and Ludwig II had it rebuilt according to the original design.*

48. *Designed after the Hall of Mirrors at Versailles,* ▷ *this gallery is slightly longer than the original, perhaps because Ludwig wanted it to be larger than that built by Louis XIV.*

The Pavilions of the Nymphenburg in Munich

In the gardens of the royal castle of Nymphenburg, exotic follies in a late eighteenth-century manner.

The Nymphenburg, the palace of the Electors of Bavaria, is today surrounded by the city of Munich, although it was constructed in the seventeenth century as a summer residence in the country. Three pavilions nearby, of all the structures built in Bavaria by the royal Wittelsbach family, reflect the happiest blend of French refinement and German sensitivity. Two, the Pagodenburg and the Badenburg, were designed by Josef Effner, the third, the Amalienburg, by François de Cuvilliès.

Beginning in the high Middle Ages, the Wittelsbachs, who came from a Bavarian place with this name, ruled Bavaria for ten centuries. Much power and many intermarriages turned this royal family into a race apart. From the Elector Ferdinand Marie, who reigned from 1651 to 1679 and built Nymphenburg for his wife Adélaïde of Savoy following the birth of their son Maximilian Emmanuel, to Ludwig II in the nineteenth century, the Wittelsbachs had a hereditary passion for building.

The Pagodenburg

The Pagodenburg was the work of Josef Effner, a Bavarian architect who had studied in Paris and had been asked by Maximilian Emmanuel to embellish Nymphenburg, which his mother had particularly liked. Maximilian Emmanuel had married Maria Antonia, daughter of the Holy Roman Emperor, Leopold I. An ally of Louis XIV of France in the War of the Spanish Succession, he was defeated by the Austrians and obliged to withdraw to the Netherlands until Louis XIV's victories secured his return to Bavaria in 1714. Shortly after that time he asked Effner to design a

Chinese pavilion based on the Trianon de Porcelaine for his wife. The Trianon de Porcelaine at Versailles had been destroyed by Louis XIV to make way for the Grand Trianon, but it remained a model throughout Europe when the fashion for chinoiserie prevailed in the eighteenth century. Maximilian Emmanuel may have also intended the pavilion as a tribute to his illustrious ally who had just died. Begun in 1716, the Pagodenburg was completed in 1719.

Built by a pond among the trees in the park of the Nymphenburg, it is a classical

49. *In the park at the palace of Nymphenburg is the Magdalenen Klause, a pavilion dedicated to death among others dedicated to life.*

pavilion with two floors; polygonal in shape, its exterior does not resemble a pagoda. However, all the interior decorations are done in the eighteenth-century chinoiserie style and agreeably combined with Corinthian pilasters and classical architectural elements. The walls of the stairway and the landing are decorated with imitation Delft tile with Chinese patterns; the door panels and walls of the drawing rooms on the upper floor are painted with black lacquer and adorned with flowers, foliage and exotic birds, a style that is the product of nostalgia for distant places. This tendency, also evident in baroque aesthetics, was to become dominant in the eighteenth century. The Pagodenburg is as much Chinese as baroque, with its *trompe-l'œil* decoration, its cane furniture, and its Chinese cabinets. For once the hereditary nostalgia of the Wittelsbachs did not appear eccentric but coincided with the taste of the period then dawning. A delight in chinoiserie was to sweep Europe.

The Badenburg

In 1718 the Wittelsbachs were eager to show that they were wealthy aristocrats with a passion for building. Although the Pagodenburg was not yet finished, Maximilian Emmanuel asked Effner to design an agreeable pavilion to be used for leisure and relaxation. The Badenburg, named for its indoor pool, was built in the park of Nymphenburg on a body of water between 1718 and 1721. It may be described as an exercise in Italian virtuosity. The ground floor of the pavilion, which has an attic with small oval windows above the French doors, contains baroque reception rooms with lavish stucco decoration and Roman busts made of marble and porphyry. A large restless and pompous fresco by the Venetian painter Jacopo Amigoni diverts, rather than satisfies, the eye.

On the first floor are two adjoining bedrooms, the one, baroque, the other "Chinese," which are variants of each other because the baroque and Oriental styles are used in a complementary manner. Eugenio d'Ors detected in the baroque of Northern Europe "the confluent of an oceanic and Far-Eastern inspiration," in which Holland played the same role for the North as Portugal for the South, a radiating point of diffusion. The "Chinese" bedroom with Louis XV paneling and stucco decoration is decorated with wallpaper depicting Chinese figures; one of the panels supposedly represents an Emperor of China. The other bedroom is Louis XV in style or, if one prefers the term, "baroque-rococo," a certain form of Louis XV style popular in France and

Austria and one of the historical and regional variations of baroque. However, the main element at the Badenburg is the pool under a gallery made of wrought-iron balustrades and marble pilasters. This pool is decorated with blue and white Delft tile and stucco moldings.

The Amalienburg

The Amalienburg, a hunting lodge, was begun by François de Cuvilliès the Elder in 1734 for Maria Amalia, wife of Charles Albert (reigned 1726-45), the son of Maximilian Emmanuel. The largest of the three Nymphenburg pavilions, it consists of a central section, flanked by two wings, in which four high windows are surmounted by stucco decorations. The roof bears, like a crown, a belvedere with a wrought-iron balcony with the initials of the Electress; from here the guests were able to shoot pheasants.

Charles Albert and his wife had little opportunity to enjoy their delightful pavilion which was completed in 1739. After he was elected emperor under the name of Charles VII in 1742, Maria Theresa of Austria, daughter of Charles VI, invaded Bavaria; Charles Albert returned only with the help of Frederick II of Prussia in 1744, a year before his death.

The main entrance of the Amalienburg is decorated with a graceful stucco frieze by Johann Baptist Zimmermann and the façade is embellished by Ionic columns. Inside, the Blue Salon is decorated with rococo motifs, silver on a white background. The Yellow Salon is also highly decorated and recalls the style which Marie de Medicis made fashionable in France and which the Italian architect of Vincenza, Andrea Palladio, the successor of Bramante and Michelangelo as architect on the construction of Saint Peter's in Rome, had created in Italy. The Amalienburg in its overly decorated style calls to mind grottoes and rocks which are not in the least natural. This architectural ambiguity has led some German critics to describe this style as "mannerist" and others to describe it as "mannerist baroque." This excess in decoration in the Blue Salon is consciously increased by the play of mirrors. On each side of this circular room are smaller rooms, four on one side and three on the other. In one of these, the "Dogs' Room," the artist painted *trompe-l'œil* kennels against which real dogs were known to break their noses. Such mock realism and deceit, excluded from art, are rustic amusements for royalty.

The kitchen was on the other side; its walls were covered with blue and white Delft tiles, like those of the Badenburg bath (blue and

63

Germany

white were the heraldic colors of Bavaria). The tiles depict "Chinese" scenes popular at the time. Blue and white chinoiseries also decorate the ceiling.

In addition to the three pavilions surrounding the Nymphenburg, there is a chapel, the Magdalenen Klause. This imitation Byzantine ruin with artificial cracks designed by Effner for Maximilian Emmanuel prefigured the fashion of ruins, which was to sweep Europe and which romantic nostalgia carried to an excess. Charles Albert's son died leaving no heir but a distant cousin, whose own son, Maximilian Joseph, was to become (by the grace of Napoleon) King of Bavaria. The latter's son, Ludwig I, the lover of Lola Montez, was present at the first performance of *Tristan*, the composer of which infatuated his grandson, Ludwig II.

Whether for Lola or their impeccable wives, the Wittelsbachs continued to build. After Charles Albert, Maximilian Joseph altered Cuvilliès's Nymphenburg. Baroque and rococo then went out of fashion. Two generations of the new line of the family, who attached the Palatinate to Bavaria, were too preoccupied with their Napoleonic relationships for architectural ventures. Ludwig I, the second Bavarian ruler to enjoy title of king, was a naïve admirer of Greece and Rome. He commissioned Romano-Byzantine buildings and brought the neoclassical period to Germany, before yielding to the pressure of the 1848 barricades caused by his relationship with Lola Montez and abandoning his throne. His grandson, the future Swan Prince, was the handsome Ludwig II, whom lovelorn ladies gathered to watch. He, however, had architectural aspirations of a different kind and was to carry the urge to build to its extreme.

50. *The Amalienburg, in the park of the Nymphenburg, was begun in 1734 for Maria Amalia, wife of Charles* *Albert. Guests shot pheasants from the belvedere on top of this hunting lodge.* 50

51. *Falcon hunting near the* ▷
Nymphenburg. In the right fore-
ground are hooded falcons. The
heron shown will be used as
game.

52. *The Amalienburg. The yel-*
low salon is decorated with paint-
ings of hunting scenes framed
in silver and gold paneling. ▽

51

52

53. *The Amalienburg. Close* ▷
to the state apartments is a
dogs' kennel walled with imi-
tation Delft and decorated with
trompe-l'œil painting.

53

54. *The blue and silver grand*
salon, a rococo masterpiece at
the Amalienburg.

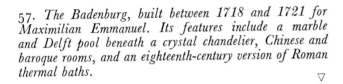

55. *The Amalienburg. A salon decorated with plaster molding celebrates the hunts of the Great Electors of Bavaria.*

56. *The Magdalenen Klause. Among many pavilions ▷ devoted to the pleasures of life, this sober building is dedicated to death, as insurance against the wrath of the gods. The cracks in the walls are intended to simulate the damage of the earthquake of judgment day.*

57. *The Badenburg, built between 1718 and 1721 for Maximilian Emmanuel. Its features include a marble and Delft pool beneath a crystal chandelier, Chinese and baroque rooms, and an eighteenth-century version of Roman thermal baths.*
▽

56

57

Next pages:
58. *The Badenburg. The marble bath, tiled in Delft. From the balcony one could speak with the noblemen while they were taking their bath.*

59. *The Amalienburg. Europe's most beautiful kitchen. Guests were received here while the food was being prepared.*

60. *Preceding the bath, the main entrance hall at the Badenburg. White stucco, gilt consoles, mirrors, and small circular windows to admit light. A pretentious setting for enlightened cleanliness.*

61. *The Pagodenburg. On the outside a Trianon, on the inside a Chinese fantasy.*

62. *The Pagodenburg. The blue salon: Delft tiles, Chinese ceiling painted in* trompe-l'œil, *blue and white rococo fur-* niture. *The room reflects a refined decor for life in the country.*

63. *A lacquered salon in the Pagodenburg pavilion. The furniture was designed specially for the room.*

63

62

64. *Apartment at the Pagodenburg. A black-lacquer commode on a floor of marquetry, lacquer and brocade on the walls. Maximilian Emmanuel, Maria Antonia, for whom the Pagodenburg was built, and Ludwig II were members of the Bavarian royal family who stayed here.*

64

Pommersfelden

Near the home of the author Ernst Hoffmann, a castle worthy of his tales.

The German composer and author Ernst Hoffmann lived and wrote his tales in Bamberg, a few miles from a château which even today seems to have emerged from one of his fantastic stories. This illusion is created by the house's exaggerated size, many rooms, and air of ostentation.

Built between 1711 and 1718, Pommersfelden has remained in the possession of the family which initiated it and today belongs of Count Karl von Schönborn-Wiesentheid. Because it is still private property, the castle has retained a family air and not been turned into a museum.

The Elector of Mainz, Prince-Archbishop of Bamberg, Lothar Franz von Schönborn (1655-1729), described by contemporary sources as a "person attracting sympathy, full of life and a great lord down to his fingertips," was the initiator of this castle. His library, still preserved, indicates the scope of his intellectual interests. Many theoretical works provided him with information about the architectural principles fashionable at that time in Austria, Bohemia, Italy, France, Holland, and England. By choosing architects and personally supervising his projects, he laid the basis of Rhineland-Franconian baroque, a synthesis of the rather heavy Italo-Bohemian baroque and the more classical French baroque.

The Prince-Elector was also interested in gardens which were an essential element of any baroque residence, and his gardens at Seehof, Favorite, Gaibach, and Pommersfelden, are part of the history of landscape decoration. Evidence of their beauty can be found today only in prints as the gardens themselves have been the victims of war, changes in fashion, and increased maintenance costs. This is true for the gardens at Pommersfelden, the ornate fountain projects which, considered too expensive, were modified by the Prince-Elector.

The central wing of the castle, designed by the architect of the Court of Bamberg, Johann Dientzenhofer, juts out into the courtyard. The great column-decorated façade enhances the powerful effect of the castle but hides the most ornate item in the building, the staircase designed by the Prince-Elector and built by Johann Lucas von Hildebrandt. Although the first in date of baroque staircases, it attains a state of perfection which makes it one of the most fascinating achievements of German baroque and is surrounded on four sides by three tiers of arcades. The immense vault with its richly colored fresco by Johann Rudolf Byss, a painter from Prague, rests on the arches supported by the pillars of the upper gallery.

In the middle of the fresco stands Phoebus Apollo on his sun chariot surrounded by other

65. *The Marble Hall is the main reception room at Pommersfelden.*

Germany

gods of ancient Olympus. In the *trompe-l'œil* painting by which Giovanni Marchini continued the arcades, groups of men and animals represent the four continents. Leaning on the balustrade, the painter seems to be examining the guests ascending the great staircase. Its dual flight of stairs rises in three sections to the second floor, where an entry room, the ceiling of which is crowned with an oval opening, leads to the two-storied Marble Hall. The walls of this immense formal hall are divided by pillars and columns of false red-brown marble. The cornice surrounding them frames one of the most beautiful ceilings in the castle. The rich decoration of the plaster work is by Daniel Schenk, and the sumptuously colored frescoes, symbolizing temporal government, are by Johann Franz Michael Rottmayer von Rosenbrunn.

The upper walls above the windows contain circular windows that diffuse round patches of light onto the multicolored marble floor. Thousands of visitors now attend concerts given every summer by young musicians in this hall formerly created for banquets and receptions.

Under the Marble Hall is the Sala Terrena, a vision of a subterranean world. Frames and strips of multicolored gems, frosted glass, and shining shellwork cover the walls and the ceiling. Ornamental surfaces covered with shells enhance the fairy-tale atmosphere. Large marble vases and fountains are placed on bases made of sparkling stones. The cornice is decorated with garlands of flowers and leaves made of shells. Characters from the *Commedia dell'Arte*, made of plaster, adorn the ceiling and recall the fantastic world of Hoffmann's tales. Four immense iron candelabra hanging from the ceiling like torches, double gilded arms emerging from the walls, strange shells, and colored globes heighten the fantastic luxury of this room. Crystal stalactites and frosted glass also hang from the ceiling and flakes of mica cover the ceiling and walls. This creates a fairy-tale vision in which snow and cold seem to have engulfed the decoration and left the role of counterpoint to the fires in the large fireplaces.

The castle and this banquet hall seem to have been abandoned suddenly, as if touched by the traditional spell of all fairy tales written by Hoffmann or Charles Perrault. The false white marble statues in the corners, made by Burkard Zammels and larger than nature, represent the four seasons and the four elements. The statues of water and fire come straight out of a romantic opera. Only eyes moving back and forth and smoke pouring from the mouths of the caryatids and masks on the walls are lacking to this animistic world to make it a replica of a motion-picture set. This subterranean room seems to have been waiting since time immemorial for the arrival of legendary lovers, finally reunited after impossible adventures in a setting which proclaims its magical character through decoration derived from opposing seasons.

On either side of the Sala Terrena, frescoes illustrate the opposition between the static and the moving. Painted vaults are filled with collapsing buildings engulfing men. The spirit of the baroque seems to be recalling the fragility of material things. The world of illusion continues in Ferdinand Plitzner's Hall of Mirrors with its floor of inlaid precious wood and its walls of inlaid walnut in which cabinets contain part of the large collection of Far Eastern porcelain. The state tables, now in the Treasury, formerly contained the best pieces of this collection—cups and vases sculpted of multicolored agate, limpid crystal, translucent amber and ivory, horns of ibex, and shells. Among the finely sculpted crystals are two beautiful pieces by the glassmaker of Kassel, Gondelach, one of which is equaled only in collections in Moscow and Rosenborg.

Pommersfelden can, therefore, be considered the realization of a dream, a fugitive idea of its builder which arose because "a caprice cannot be made to wait" and was created for fêtes and the life of society. We do not know whether the Prince-Elector organized an impressive reception, even during the most important phases of construction such as the laying of the cornerstone and the consecration of the altar marking the end of work. His political responsibilities kept him from the castle.

The reproduction of the castle in engravings by Salomon Kleiner shows that the Prince-Elector was conscious of having made an important contribution to the history of German architecture through his work as a builder, of having indicated the artistic possibilities of the empire, and of having defined his position as the first prince of the empire after the Emperor.

The castle was above all destined to house the great painting collection of its owner, a collection of which he could write in 1715 to his favorite nephew Frederick Karl, Vice Chancellor of the empire in Vienna: "Only the imperial gallery and the gallery of the Elector of the Palatinate can compare with mine." The Prince-Elector corresponded with many contemporary artists, and diplomats and special agents served as his buyers. In 1719 his catalog listed 482 paintings. This was the first such catalog published in Germany. Financial difficulties unfortunately obliged his heirs to sell several paintings in the nineteenth century. Rembrandt's *The Seeress Hanna* and *Saint Paul in Prison*, Rubens' *David Playing the Harp* and *Saint Francis of Assisi*, and Dürer's *Jacob Müffel* were sold as well as paintings of lesser value. In the nineteenth century the collection at Pommersfelden was enriched by the addition of the collection from Gaibach, which also belonged to the Prince-Elector and now contains more than 600 paintings, including works by Rubens, Titian, Van Dyck, Van der Helst, Gio-

Germany

vanni da Bologna, the Breughels and painters of the schools of Rembrandt and Dürer, as well as von Momper, Liss, Honthorst, de Heem, Le Nain, and Pesne. The collection also contains Italian seventeenth-century works representative of all schools as well as remarkable paintings of flowers. Pommersfelden represented all the trends and fashions of an eighteenth-century German princely residence. Large paintings are still hung beside and over each other in the two-storied gallery as they were originally in imitation of the gallery of the Archduke Leopold in Brussels, whom the Prince-Elector visited on his trips. Other rooms, formerly inhabited by the Prince, also contain valuable paintings as well as beautiful furniture. The white, pink and gold fresco decorating the dining room shows Ganymede, the cup-bearer of the gods, surrounded by plaster cupids giving a concert. The center of the Nymphenburg porcelain table with its green hedges and white rustic figures recall the charm of the baroque gardens today replaced by meadows and woods.

The Prince-Elector's library was also moved from Gaibach to Pommersfelden in the 1830's with its papyrus manuscripts, 400 other valuable manuscripts, and priceless incunabula. All fields of knowledge are represented among these 10,000 volumes by the most important works published at that time.

Next pages :
67-68. *Two views of the grotto, or Sala Terrena.*

66. *The baroque staircase at Pommersfelden.* ▷

The Park of Schwetzingen

A palace with a thermal bath covered with amethysts, an erotic garden, a fountain of birds, and an extravagant park where Elisabeth Charlotte, Princess Palatine, spent her childhood.

Love of nature inspired the gardens of the castle of Schwetzingen located near Baden. Created in two different phases after 1758, they combine a characteristically French perspective with an inspiration seemingly derived from the park in Goethe's *Die Wahlverwandtschaften*. The gardens are dedicated to love, and contain grottoes, fountains, groves peopled with mythological statues, and false pavilions decorated with amethysts and rock crystals. As a concession to the taste of the period in which it was created, the complex also has an erotic garden and a bird fountain, a fantasy which has attracted people from the entire world. (Such a bird fountain also once existed at Versailles.) The park qualifies the castle of Schwetzingen for a place among the dream palaces.

Although Schwetzingen is a late eighteenth-century castle it is furnished with light-colored wood furniture with bands of darker inlay. Its striking rooms are hung with wallpaper of the romantic period representing fabrics.

Schwetzingen was the summer residence of the Electors of the Palatinate; Heidelberg was their home. Hoping to ensure peace along the Rhine, the Elector Karl-Ludwig married his daughter (Elisabeth Charlotte, known as Lise-lotte) to Philippe d'Orléans, "Monsieur" as he was called, Louis XIV's brother. Elisabeth d'Orléans, the Princess Palatine, was famous for her letters written to royal relations throughout Europe.

Liselotte was to leave her Rhineland homes for Versailles and Saint-Cloud, where Monsieur was building a residence which might prove more handsome than her father's. By marrying Philippe d'Orléans, who did not like women, she assumed the place of Henrietta Stuart (the beloved sister of Charles II of England immortalized by Bishop Jacques Bénigne Bossuet in a celebrated funeral oration). Henrietta was said to have been poisoned by Monsieur's favorite, the Chevalier de Lorraine, younger son of the Comte d'Harcourt, Master of the Horse. Liselotte, who regretted not being a boy, loved hunting and strenuous exercise. Raised in the forests of Germany, she shared some of their rugged qualities: "No one was ever uglier with more spirit and cheerfulness," said Duke Louis de Saint-Simon. She was sacrificed for the Palatinate, dangerously located between France and the Empire and in need of Louis XIV's protection.

Monsieur was thirty; Liselotte saw him

69. *The Fountain of Birds in the park at Schwetzingen by Nicolas de Pigage.*

as "small and plump with very black hair and eyebrows..." According to Saint-Simon, Monsieur described her as having "the face and boorishness of a Swiss"; and he despaired: "How on earth can I sleep with her?" He was slight and effeminate, excessively made-up, perfumed, and covered with jewels. She writes in her letters that she succeeded in getting "him used to her ugliness" while she became accustomed to his favorites, at least in the beginning. She transferred her affection to Louis XIV but could not bear the king's wife, Mme de Maintenon. The things which she wrote about Mme de Maintenon in her letters to Heidelberg (she called her "the great man's old garbage") were the cause of her final disgrace, although Louis XIV had at first enjoyed her candor. She was no longer invited to the king's hunts.

When her brother, the Elector Charles IX, died without an heir in 1685, Louis XIV claimed his lands on the left bank of the Rhine as the inheritance of his sister-in-law. He occupied its towns, and Liselotte was much upset. She was told by a man from Heidelberg of the savage "scorched earth" policy of the French commander Louvois. She tried to intervene on behalf of her country, but in vain.

Mannheim and Heidelberg were sacked in 1689 and atrocities were committed. "What annoys me," wrote the Princess Palatine, "is their use of my name to dupe the wretched inhabitants of the Palatinate. Monsieur has told me that contributions were levied in my name and the poor people must think that I am profiting from their misfortune..."

The furniture of her brother, the Elector, was sold and his silver melted down. The celebrated tapestries and pictures of Heidelberg were brought to Monsieur. Yet "I only get a hundred pistoles a month," wrote Liselotte, "... Monsieur never gives me a penny..." The walls of the gallery of Saint-Cloud were adorned with works pirated from the castle of Heidelberg which she had loved so much. The Elector's best paintings decorated the rooms of the Chevalier de Lorraine.

Eight years later, Louis XIV was obliged to hand back all the territory which he had seized, except Strasbourg. The liberated Palatinate rose again from its ruins, but Heidelberg was not rebuilt. Madame's family devoted all their attention to their properties at Mannheim and Schwetzingen.

At the summer residence of Schwetzingen, the main vista is produced by a crescent-shaped mass of greenery—a bower of foliage 1,000 feet long with nothing else in sight but a vault of trees opening on large fountains. At the end of this walk can be seen the court theater, used every summer for a drama festival. The large fountains are preceded by small fountains in the middle of which are cupids holding jets of water, similar to fountains often found in Germany. Several such jets tracing patterns in the air, like complicated fireworks, provide an impression of perpetual movement.

The first of the large fountains is classical, with statues and fountains throwing their water high into the sky. The second is characteristic of Schwetzingen, two large stags at bay spew water into a small pool on the edge of a forest, the perspective of which is broken only by the vista of the park. The third fountain is framed by a romantic landscape. On the right is a winding, artificial stream, one of the two branches of which symbolizes the female, and the other the male. In a thicket the god Pan plays on a rock above a fountain.

Near the grove of the Temple of Apollo behind the bath house is the Fountain of Birds, Nicolas de Pigage's masterpiece. Lead birds are placed along the edge of an immense circular arbor open to the sky. From the beak of each pours a stream of water that falls into a central pool and forms an arch of water under which visitors can walk. In the middle of this pool an owl with its wings outstretched over its prey serves as a central fountain. The many streams of water, under which visitors can pass without getting wet, create a refreshing room in the summer. A similar folly can be seen at the Grand Trianon in a painting of an old view of the park at Versailles during a *fête*, although the birds are not placed in an arbor but in a recess. Countless English and German

prints show the Schwetzingen Fountain of Birds visited during the romantic period by women wearing crinolines and men in top hats. This architectural folly was, and still is, one of the most curious in Europe.

The bath house (1773), next to the Fountain of Birds, has an exterior that recalls small eighteenth-century houses of the Ile-de-France, although the inside is typical of German baroque. In the circular hall marble consoles are supported by large golden eagles. On each side of the niches occupied by gilded statues, crystal chandeliers rest on small wooden brackets. On either side of the entrance are small salons that lead to the masterpiece of the house, the bath. The bath is surrounded by white stucco draperies. A monumental urn pours water into the pool, which is reached by descending a few steps. The sculptured stone of the walls represents nymphs carrying water against a background of rock formations. The doors are inlaid with mirrors set with amethysts; the pillars are decorated with cupids playing with dolphins; the ceiling is adorned with mirrors, stucco moldings, and inlaid amethysts around a central decorative element of scallop shells and coral. The window recesses are covered with fragments of amethysts. The bath is illuminated by light filtering through an oval window and by a lantern. The room sparkles with gilded mirrors, mauve stones, and uncut amethysts which look like quartz.

Germany

Leaving the pavilion, visitors pass in front of the Temple of Apollo over cascades and moss. They cross a stone crescent, the steps of which are decorated with sphinxes crouched over books. This leads to the main walk and then to the lake. Not far to the left are the ruins of the Temple of Mercury and the minarets of a mosque.

The folly of the park of Schwetzingen was one of the last fantasies of a period during which the nobility played at being shepherdesses at the Trianon, or pretended to be French in Saint Petersburg. Masked balls were as popular in Venice as at Drottningholm and in London. The rites of hospitality, which had been traditionally perpetuated from the sixteenth century, were increasingly and recklessly extravagant. Life at that time was spent in war or festivity, and the follies offered for pleasure were justified by those offered for death.

70. *A statue of a faun overlooking a garden dedicated to love and sentiment.*

71

72

73

74

Preceding pages:
71. *Fountain of Stags.*

72. *The bath house seen from the Fountain of Birds.*

73. *Stags at bay.*

74. *White walls with candelabra and consoles supported by griffins decorate a salon that leads to the bath.*

75. *The gardens possess two artificial streams, one male (shown here), the other female. The garden is dedicated to Pan.*
▽

76

76. *A sphinx near the Temple of Apollo.*

75

80

The female stream.

77

78

78. *The baroque theater at Schwetzingen, one of the most beautiful in Germany, is now used for an annual festival.*

79

79. *The Temple of Apollo is at the top of a cascade.*

80. *A long vista in the park at Schwetzingen. From the first two fountains in front of the castle a pond can be seen as well as a view of the romantic countryside.*

82. *Detail of the entrance to the bath house.*

81. *The bath's ceiling, decorated with precious stones, stucco, and mirrors.*

83. *The bath is surrounded by white stucco draperies and urns.*

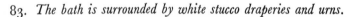

84. *Two nymphs carrying water.*

85. *A wall simulating the rock* ▷ *formations of a grotto. Stucco nymphs, doors of gilded wood, amethyst, mirrors, and an eighteenth - century baroque lantern comprise a rich decor.*

85

The Royal Pavilion at Brighton

A palace, which Coleridge described in *Kubla Khan, or a Vision in a Dream,* was built by an incorrigible eccentric for a beautiful widow, Mrs. Fitzherbert, while he waited to accede to the throne of England.

The Royal Pavilion in Brighton, on the south coast of England, is a curious assemblage of domes and minarets commissioned by King George IV. In 1786, while still Prince of Wales, George bought a small country house in this former military port, then little more than a village because of the silting of the harbor. For forty years this property was to be the crucible of his dreams. As Regent, he transformed Brighton into a fashionable watering place where his pavilion was the realization of the aspirations of the Regency style and English romanticism.

The Prince of Wales withdrew to Brighton in order to live pastorally, like the early eighteenth-century philosophers, and find the seclusion he needed for a secret love affair. When he was twenty-two, he met Mrs. Maria Ann Fitzherbert, commonly referred to simply as Mrs. Fitzherbert. Twice widowed and a devout Catholic, she tolerated no association outside the conventions of marriage. When she realized that she was loved by the prince, she fled to Paris.

The prince wrote to her begging her to return. She agreed, and the prince proposed that they flee together to America. Eventually they reached a compromise: she consented to marry him secretly in the prince's dining room, according to the rites of the Catholic Church.

Even before the dreams which sapped his substance assumed an architectural form, the Regent was crippled with liabilities, the heaviest of which had been contracted in his pursuit of the chaste widow. King George III flew into a rage on learning of his son's debts and proposed marriage, although he finally paid the obligations after forcing his son to begin a period of austere frugality. The prince then stopped construction of his London house and sold his stables. But where could he hide his love who would yield only where she was safe from the slander of the king's court?

During a stay in Brighton in 1783 the prince had become attached to the area and the following year he chose this town as a haven for his love affair. He sent his steward there to rent a house, and then to France to buy the appropriate furnishings. These are now in Windsor Castle and Buckingham Palace.

Since the prince had sold his carriages with his stables, he and his wife had to travel to Brighton in a rented coach. Were his wife, who was still called Mrs. Fitzherbert, to sleep

86. *The Regent, later George IV of Great Britain, a man who spent his time pursuing flights of fancy while awaiting his rise to power.*

under the same roof as the prince, a scandal would ensue. Therefore, he rented for her a villa on the River Steine, along the village promenade, next to the home of the Duke of Marlborough. In 1786 the prince rented a small gentleman's manor which was just outside the town.

In 1787, his passion for building appeared for the first time and he began to transform this manor which eventually became the famous Pavilion. The gentry became inquisitive once he moved in. After visiting the prince, Elizabeth Collet, then twenty-four, described in her diary certain peculiarities of his bed. The bed was reached by a few steps and was against a wall covered by a mirror which, to all appearances, allowed the Regent to contemplate the sea without arising. Another room was decorated with particularly amusing caricatures.

Within five months Henry Holland, an architect to the London aristocracy, had transformed this house into a residence in the then fashionable Greco-Roman style with a central rotunda and two flanking wings, one of which was the original house. The circular drawing room was decorated with Ionic columns supporting a dome reminiscent of a Greek temple. The home of this clandestine couple eventually became the prototype for future bow-windowed Regency houses.

The furniture was bought in Paris by the prince's steward and went well with the many French decorative touches inspired by Holland's personal taste. The corridors were painted French blue, the staircase bright green, and the drawing room ceiling gray and white. An Aubusson carpet, a branched chandelier, and a *trompe-l'œil* painting by Biagio Rebecca decorated the drawing room. The Regent spent many hours in the large billiard room. The lawn in front of the house required continuous attention. The only separation between the house and the River Steine was a ditch which formed a barrier without interfering with the view. The dining room was reportedly like an oven, and once the fire was lit it became as "hot as hell" as a guest once remarked to the playwright Sheridan. Sheridan quipped that it was always good to have a taste in this world of what awaits us in the next.

The drama, however, was just beginning. Despite economies which the prince probably considered draconian, his debts were by no means eliminated and his rent was a year overdue. George III was well informed of all events at Brighton. He even knew that the prince's affection for Mrs. Fitzherbert was no longer in its early stages.

One winter evening the Prince of Wales was abruptly summoned to Windsor. He departed from Brighton leaving Mrs. Fitzherbert trembling. The prince arrived for dinner at Windsor. A strange soul, in many ways quite modern, still seeking change, increasingly intense and very acute but unable to satisfy his dulled sensitivity, yet peremptory in politics like his father and absolutist in face of the Revolution and Napoleon, he did not at all suspect his father's imminent demands. As they were about to sit down for dinner, the king appeared, lunged at his son and, grabbing his throat, banged his head against the wall. Confused and upset by such a display of hateful fury, the prince burst into tears. George III ejaculated a series of enigmatic phrases among which were some reasonable refusals and demands. He would no longer pay the prince's debts; he demanded that his son marry in keeping with his rank and that there be an heir to the throne. The king's excessive agitation, his incoherent speech and his brutality worried his entourage; intrigues were contrived; and Parliament demanded that a Regency be established in the name of the prodigal son. George III, however, overcame his illness and it was no longer wise for the Prince of Wales to dream of non-existent castles.

Then George III intervened again, and designated his cousin, Princess Caroline of Brunswick, as the future wife of the prince. This choice was made as much to regulate the prince's financial matters as to ensure the future of the dynasty. The princess was the daughter of Charles William Ferdinand, Duke of Brunswick-Wolfenbuttel, the author of a notorious manifesto which, sent from Coblenz to France, provoked an insurrection and led to the downfall of Louis XVI.

In London drawing rooms it was whispered that the marriage was not the work of just George III but rather that it had been planned by the Duchess of Jersey. The prince was thirty-three and would soon be king. The ambitious duchess could think of no better way of separating him from Mrs. Fitzherbert than to marry him to a princess whom she knew he would not love; she would be his consolation, or so she thought.

The lavish court marriage took place on April 8, 1795. After the ceremony, the prince decided to return to Brighton with his new wife to supervise work on the Pavilion. The entire Brighton household was reorganized, and the royal couple moved into the Marlborough house with the Duchess of Jersey as lady-in-waiting to Princess Caroline. Soon pregnant and feeling neglected, Caroline fled to the countryside outside of Brighton, where in January of 1796 she gave birth to a daughter, Charlotte, the future first wife of King Leopold of Belgium.

Liberated, the prince recovered his taste for construction and abandoned the Duchess of Jersey to move back into the Pavilion. He was once again possessed by his fantasies, a taste for luxury, and an almost feminine yearning for property and material things. He set about rebuilding everything, his love life as

England

well as the Pavilion. The day after the birth of Princess Charlotte, he informed Caroline that their separation was definitive. After another three days had passed, he handwrote a will naming Mrs. Fitzherbert as sole beneficiary and referring to her as "my wife, the wife of my heart and soul." By this time, she had had her secret marriage legitimized by the Pope, then Napoleon's prisoner in France; and in the eyes of the Catholic Church the widow Fitzherbert was indeed the wife of Augustus Frederick George, Prince of Wales. The morganatic couple celebrated the good news with an extravagant party that marked a return to the festive life of Brighton and signaled a rejuvenation which would surely benefit the Pavilion itself.

The Pavilion and those who were drawn there by a baroque dream resembled each other. Whether French, Greco-Roman, Chinese, or Indian, the Pavilion of His Royal Highness amazed contemporaries and dazzled them with its extravagance.

Abandoned, Caroline wandered across Europe, fell in love with an Italian courier, whom she made a count, rebelled against her husband then king and tried in vain to turn the people of London against him.

Between 1801 and 1804 George commissioned the architect Robinson, Holland's nephew, to add two wings to the Pavilion which was fast becoming a royal palace. Robinson constructed two cornered oval wings to house the dining room and the drawing studio. He was a landscape designer and thus had a taste for the picturesque which prompted him to add pagoda canopies above all the windows.

Chinoiseries had been introduced into England ten years earlier when Dutch artists decorated one of the rooms of the prince's London residence, Carlton House, in the Chinese style. At the time, George paid little attention to this innovation. By 1790 lacquer ware, imported for many years from Denmark, was well known in England. Chinese pavilions, pagodas, and those gardens called "Chinese" by the English and "English" by the French were found at Schoenbrunn Palace in Vienna, in Bavaria and in France, where Louis XIV had replaced the Trianon de Porcelaine with Mansart's Grand Trianon. A number of albums, some whimsical and others scholarly such as the album published by Sir William Chambers, who designed the Kew Palace pagoda, provided artists with aquatint plans and representations of Chinese architecture. Paul Sandby designed a majestic junk for George III to use on the Thames. In the early years of the nineteenth century the Gothic, classical, rococo, and Chinese styles were indiscriminately mixed; people did not wish, did not know how, or perhaps were unable to choose. Painted wallpaper reproducing Chinese scenes and gardens alive with exotic birds, flowers, and insects whose names were unknown to westerners decorated the homes of such ladies as Mrs. Elizabeth Montague. Chippendale designed the fantastic "Chinese" bed now exhibited in the Victoria and Albert Museum; tea had finally found a definitive place in English society; and Chinese was the reigning fashion. In his drive for change and renewal, the Prince of Wales made this style his and decided that the Pavilion would be Chinese.

Everything in Chinese style in Carlton House, the prince's London home, was transported to Brighton. Among those objects were tables designed by Holland in 1790 and a marble mantelpiece adorned with Chinese figures which was placed in the gallery, where the walls were covered with Chinese paper. During the years 1802 and 1803 Grace & Sons furnished the prince with several lacquered cabinets, couches, chairs, bamboo stools, and a large number of porcelain pieces, bowls, statues, and vases. The prince bought anything Chinese: miniature junks and pagodas, costumes, swallow nests, masks, tobacco, and razors. Costumed Chinese mannequins stood in the gallery holding wands from which lanterns were suspended. The accounts kept by Grace & Sons show that the prince bought objects of little value as readily as genuine works of art.

The music room had painted dragon columns and a ceiling with a Louis Barzago painting representing heaven in the Italian style. The armchairs were decorated in a Chi-nese style and are now at Buckingham Palace with the Regent's piano. The walls of the drawing room were hung with Chinese-patterned India paper and bamboo paneling. The ceiling of the drawing room was supported by painted columns. With the passage of time the Chinese decoration became increasingly elaborate. In 1817 Robert Jones painted Chinese portraits and framed them in bamboo before hanging them in the banquet hall. He also designed a rosewood sideboard with legs supported by dragon-shaped feet. This room also had an immense marble fireplace (now in Buckingham Palace) ornamented with Chinese figures in ormolu. Large panels simulating bamboo decorated the gallery. The lamps and globes of the chandeliers looked like long-petaled water-lilies. The prince's bedroom had a canopied bed with four black lacquered posts adorned with gilded Chinese motifs and was furnished with a handsome black and gold lacquered cabinet, a swing mirror, and imitation bamboo chairs. Even the pillars in the large kitchen looked Chinese with their shafts which had been transformed into the slender trunks of coconut palms topped with a cluster of cut sheet-metal fronds which curved down from the ceiling.

A fantastic dream nourished itself. It inspired the raising of blocks of masonry, drilling, digging, and reconstructing. From the other side of the globe furniture and objects which by their shape, carved details, varieties of molding, and colors would delight the future king were ordered.

Once the inside was thoroughly Chinese the exterior had to be similarly transformed. The prince explained to all his frowning and wary friends that he would tolerate nothing typical of France because he was afraid of being accused of Jacobinism.

After being invited to retransform the pavilion, the architect William Porden abandoned the idea of a neo-Gothic castle and made new proposals inspired by the album by Sir William Chambers: *Designs for Chinese Buildings*.

A new spirit coursed through Brighton as horse racing became as important to English society as tea. The reconstituted stables were well stocked; every morning the guests were free to use horses and carriages. After buying more land, the prince temporarily postponed the transformation of the Pavilion in order to devote himself to the construction of new stables. Napoleon's exploits had made the sea lanes unsafe and thus the necessary lumber arrived only after long delays. For this reason, the new stable building, modeled after the Halle au Blé built in Paris in 1782, was not completed until 1808. This new stable was called the Dome because of a central dome which allowed light to fall on the forty-four stalls encircling the fountain used to water the horses. On the upper floor was a ring-balcony offering access to jockeys' quarters and harness rooms.

The life of the lovers became sober and settled in this Chinese setting; as a contemporary remarked, "their love increased as did their weight." After their morning walk guests would have lunch and then relax while playing games or listening to music until afternoon tea. At eight o'clock the ladies and at eight fifteen the gentlemen would withdraw to dress for dinner. Evening etiquette required that the men stand and the ladies remain seated. They waited for the prince to enter the salon. When he arrived the ladies would stand while the prince spoke briefly to each of his guests and shook hands with newcomers and some of his closer friends before asking the ladies to be seated. When dinner was announced, he would offer his arm to the most titled of the ladies. After dinner there would be music and a light supper of sandwiches, wine, and spring water. The prince would often play patience.

Here amid his chinoiseries he must have learned of the victory at Trafalgar and the death of Nelson before people in London because of Brighton's coastal location. He must also have followed the progress of Napoleon's conquests, heard of his return from Elba, unrolled maps of Europe, and discussed the situation with Wellington. He also welcomed his daughter Charlotte for the first time when she was twelve; and here also his one great passion for Mrs. Fitzherbert gradually waned.

Among the numerous and frequent visitors

to the Pavilion was the painting connoisseur Lord Hertford who gladly advised the prince on several occasions. George was happier still to entertain Lady Hertford who was always discreet. The people of Brighton and even the royal court had become accustomed to and even accepted Mrs. Fitzherbert, who now became a screen behind which the prince hid his new infatuation.

King George III was adjudged insane and the prince was appointed Regent in 1811. When in June of the following year the Regent gave a banquet to celebrate officially his appointment, the guests were informed that they would be seated not according to their degree of intimacy with the Regent but according to their rank and nobility. Feeling the arrival of a decisive point in their relationship, Mrs. Fitzherbert asked the Regent where she was to be seated. He replied, "You know very well, madam, that you do not have a place." She answered: "None but that which you choose to give me," and left for Brighton, but not the Pavilion, never to return.

During his Regency (1811-20) a Tory cabinet directed the war against Napoleon: the Prussian campaign and Leipzig in 1813, Elba in 1814 and the victory of Waterloo on June 18, 1815. Just after Wellington's victory Humphrey Repton submitted designs for transforming the Pavilion, but it was John Nash who was commissioned to modify it into a Hindu residence.

The Regent had apparently always wished more for a Pavilion with an Indian cast than one in the then well-established Chinese style, and he once again began to dream of such a Pavilion. The English curiously seemed to confuse India and China and this developed a strong taste for what came to be called "Indian romanticism."

Nash, who was a gifted architect as well as a good friend, submitted two plans to the Regent, one of which called for a large dome above the salon and two smaller flanking domes. This plan flattered the royal client, who had been dazzled by the domed construction of his new stables, and was therefore accepted.

From 1818 to 1821 the Pavilion was Indianized. During the transformation the Regent was crowned (1820), thus assuring the necessary financial backing for the new Pavilion.

Nash and the king studied all the possible means of marrying the Chinese and Indian styles. Nash had two additional rooms constructed, covered them with tentlike roofs and linked them to the older parts of the Pavilion by installing a series of columns in the Indian style. The main entrance, simulating a festooned tent topped by a dome, was based on the sketch of a temple on the Ganges. Great sums of money were squandered while riots broke out in London and the people demanded liberal reforms.

The king's relatively modest suite included a bedroom, an anteroom, a library and a

England

bathroom. There was a similar suite above intended for a lady, perhaps Lady Hertford or the Marchioness of Conyngham. A tower was built and became known as the Clock Tower after Brighton coaches began using it to schedule their departures. Balustrades, minarets, balconies, columns, domes, and fireplaces, all in Brighton stone, made the Pavilion stand out in strong contrast to the usually somber sea and coast. The Princess of Lieven, wife of the Russian ambassador, compared the new Pavilion to a mosque or the Kremlin, describing it as "a mixture of Moorish, Tartar, Gothic and Chinese, all in stone and iron." She was appalled at its cost.

An underground passage, supposedly used by the Regent to go incognito to rendezvous or to Mrs. Fitzherbert's, was built from the Pavilion to the site of the prince's latest love, his stables and horses.

It was the Royal Pavilion that was to provide the setting for the dramatic reunion and reconciliation between George IV and his daughter Charlotte. In 1814 she had dared to defy him by refusing to marry William of Orange, an indolent and drunken boor. George had her confined to Windsor Castle until 1816, when Prince Leopold of Saxe-Coburg, the future King of Belgium, asked her hand in marriage. After receiving her in Brighton and giving his permission for the marriage, George ordered that the necessary preparations be made. His daughter was married in a ceremony which promised future happiness. Charlotte died in childbirth in 1817 and the grief-stricken George withdrew to the Pavilion to hide his sadness. After his coronation George was confined to a wheelchair. He made a final visit to the Pavilion from January to March of 1827 and then left for Windsor Castle where he remained until his death in 1830.

The Royal Pavilion became little more than a lifeless folly; Queen Victoria was never happy there; and in 1850 the town of Brighton bought the Pavilion and turned it into a showcase for chinoiseries from neighboring castles and from the Pavilion itself, which epitomized the Regency period.

The king in his last years became as insensitive to the magic of the Pavilion as he had become to the magic of a former mistress' glance or voice. For us, the eclecticism of this period epitomizes the English romantic decorative style.

87. *A modest Brighton villa was transformed into a Hindu palace containing Chinese salons and bedrooms.*

88. The Regent's Chinese chamber.

88

90. The double staircase at Brighton, with cast-iron banisters of simulated bamboo. Pink Chinese wallpaper with gray bamboo motifs. The staircase leads to the main gallery built in 1802. Today the room still contains the original Chinese statues, paper lanterns, bronze ibises, Chinese vases, teakwood consoles, and bamboo furniture. ▷

89. One of the small Chinese rooms.

89

91. *Humphrey Repton, whose taste was eclectic, contributed to the building of Brighton. When he submitted his designs for the Regent's palace, he explained that neither the Grecian nor Gothic style would harmonize with the buildings already existing: "I therefore considered," he said, "all the different styles of different countries from the conviction of the danger of attempting to invent anything entirely new. The Turkish was objectional as being a corruption of the Grecian; the Moorish as a bad model of the Gothic; the Egyptian was too cumberous for the character of a villa; the Chinese too light and trifling for the outside, however it may be applied to the interior. Thus if any known style were to be adopted no alternative remained but to combine from the architecture of Hindustan such forms as might be rendered applicable to the purpose." However, John Nash, not Repton, was chosen to undertake the actual construction, which was completed in 1821.*

91

92. *A summer pavilion at Brighton.*

92

93. The Fox and the Bust.

What a goodly figure this makes!
What a Pity that it should want Brains.
- *Aesop's Fables*

*The fox is minister of the court; the bust is of the Regent.
In the background, a caricature of the Regent's Egeria,
Mrs. Fitzherbert.*

▷

93

94. *An anti-royalist caricature. The king with gout in
Brighton looks like a comical bloated maggot and has to
be lifted onto his horse by means of a mechanical contri-
vance.*

▽

94

96

96. *Mrs. Fitzherbert by Richard Conway.*

97

A VOLUPTUARY under the horrors of Digestion.

97. *The Regent, who indulged in every pleasure, shown eating.*

◁ 95. *The banquet room, designed by John Nash. Its chandeliers foreshadow the decorative art of Louis Comfort Tiffany.*

Preceding page:
98. *The music room at Brighton, designed by John Nash in 1822. Nine gas chandeliers decorated with water lilies and dragons hang from the domed ceiling. The walls are decorated with red and gold Chinese landscapes separated by pilasters around which serpents are coiled. After dinner George IV, accompanied by seventy musicians, would come to this room and sing* Glorious Apollo *and* Mighty Conqueror *for the amusement of his guests. A turquoise Axminster rug with dragon, mandarin, and lotus motifs formerly covered the floor. Beyond this room are a series of salons with columns and bell-hung cornices.*

99. *The kitchen, from an engraving in John Nash's* Views of the Royal Pavilion *(1826). Large metal palm trees function as columns. Many for these exotic fantasies were designed by Robert Jones. William Hazlitt, who did not like Brighton, called the Pavilion* "a collection of stone pumpkins and pepper boxes. The inside is a collection of strange columns. Palm trees decorate the kitchen, clusters of bells decorate the salon and parasols made of glass serve as chandeliers."

99

100. *The kitchen at Brighton today. Nothing has changed and the French menu may still be examined.* ▽

100

Beckford and Fonthill Abbey

The dream of an author who described his diabolical fancies in *Vathek*, the first masterpiece of English Romanticism.

At Fonthill, in Wiltshire, England, there was once an estate which gave the owner the right to stand for one of the two Parliamentary seats of Shaftesbury. Two follies were built on this estate: one was the product of ambition for power, the other of ambition to realize a dream. The first, Fonthill Splendens, was built by a man who became Lord Mayor of London and led a fight against King George III; the second, Fonthill Abbey, was built in the early 1800's by the Lord Mayor's son, William Beckford, whom one of his greatest admirers, Byron, described as a "martyr to prejudice."

William Beckford, who destroyed Splendens to replace it with his necromantic abbey, was an aesthete descended from four generations of wealthy Jamaican planters. He left a singular description of the Lord Mayor's residence: "The great mansion of Fonthill which I demolished to construct a still more extraordinary edifice," he wrote, "was admirably calculated for the celebration of mysteries. The solid Egyptian Hall looking as if hewn out of a living rock, the line of apartments and apparently endless passages extending from it on either side were all vaulted..."

Beckford built for himself a palace that matched the distorted splendor of his dreams.

The towers of Fonthill built to replace Splendens were the result of much thought. Beckford's dreams of distant places and exotic life were rooted in childhood. As with King Ludwig II of Bavaria and some Austrian princes, such dreams of grandeur were generated by an intense inner life. Only a huge fortune could have realized them. Ludwig II was to be a king, and so too was Beckford, due to his income from the family's sugar estates in Jamaica. Both were able to dream and make their dreams come true, and both shared the view that they were exceptional beings. Each spent his childhood in the solitude of a palace enlivened only by the presence of tutors. As adults, they were lonely, introspective, intuitively sensitive, living out their grandiose dreams of unique, emotionally overwhelming, and often barely reciprocated friendships, and seeking impassioned love in its most varied forms.

Beckford expected everything of a young Fonthill neighbor, Lord Courtenay, a child of thirteen known as Kitty. Later, when that expectation had been disappointed, he tried to find substitutes among the peculiarly talented, including a tightrope walker, momentarily seen one evening when Beckford was middle-aged and never encountered again.

101. *The main gallery of the Gothic abbey at Fonthill, designed by John Nash for William Beckford.*

England

Beckford's life was a succession of infatuations for people curious, like him, to experience the unseen and to discover the evil implied in morality, especially in puritan morality. Here was the romantic myth of the fallen angel, who wanted to be God's peer but, unable to be so, turned against Him. Beckford's world was born with him. His mother, "the Queen-Mother," as he called her, was a member of the distinguished Hamilton family. Mrs. Beckford required her son's tutors to be exceptional, and indeed the influence of the first tutor impressed itself strongly upon the sensitive and remarkably gifted child. Beckford was born in 1760. At the age of three he was learning Latin and French (his principal literary work, *Vathek*, was written in French). At five he had music lessons from Mozart, on tour at the time in London. Years later, Beckford claimed that the air "*Non più andrai*" from *The Marriage of Figaro* was composed by him. At seven, his mother had entrusted her son to a Scotch tutor, Robert Drysdale, who introduced him to Thucydides and other classic authors. The Lord Mayor's friends were appropriately impressed. At thirteen, William was translating Homer and Cicero at sight and analyzing Locke's *Essay Concerning Human Understanding*. Shakespeare and Bacon had no secrets for him, but it appears that *The Arabian Nights* was forbidden. No matter, the library at Fonthill Splendens had plenty of books to stir the imagination —Ariosto, Ossian, Scott, and all the fashionable Oriental tales. Beckford's taste for the unfamiliar could easily be satisfied.

Lord Chatham, his godfather, wrote to William Pitt of him in 1773 that he was a "vivid young friend... compounded of the elements of air and fire."

By now Drysdale had been superseded as tutor by the Reverend John Lettice, while Sir William Chambers was instructing him in the principles of architecture and Alexander Cozens (who claimed descent from Peter the Great) in the art of watercolor and drawing. This period marked the beginning of William's rebellion against the conventions of his class. He disliked both hunting and sportsmen, and dreamed of creating, as his father had also dreamed before his death, a kingdom encircled by a wall. In the center of this domain he would raise tower upon tower... and from their tops he would gaze at the stars, like an Oriental potentate, contemptuous of mankind.

Many of his friends were twenty years older than he. William disliked sports but enjoyed solitude and the privilege of his own company. The painter George Romney shows him at the age of twenty-one, leaning against a balustrade, apparently gazing into infinity, with the air of one who dreams of being caliph or prophet, or at least of remaining foreign to the world of his time.

Alexander Cozens was soon to extend his

influence over his pupil and guide him into the purlieus of darkness. As a painter, Cozens was highly subjective, depicting landscapes washed with light and shadow, spots of color scattered over wet paper, studies of chance, spontaneous effects to arouse the imagination. Cozens represented Asia, the Caucasus, Persia, and Tartary. He was the traveler, the answer to Beckford's yearnings. Cozens initiated him into forbidden sciences, magic, and the cabala. Soon William was more than a pupil. He was a disciple. "Could I have imagined," wrote the boy, "anyone possessing such rays which transfix me? Strange, very strange that such perfect conformity can exist." When they were apart, William placed his letters "in a drawer lined with blue, the colour of the ether." Air and fire... a combination which Beckford would always pursue and which he found in Cozens.

The Reverend Lettice, however, was aware of their relationship and discreetly warned his mother and Lord Chatham of the pupil's fascination with his tutor. Beckford was sent off to visit Hamilton cousins in Switzerland, accompanied by Lettice.

Lake Geneva was at that time the resort of European intellectual society and, in particular, of those who were interested in the philosophy of illuminism, which Beckford was quick to discover. He was seventeen and everything interested him. He wrote to Cozens on September 12, 1777, that "the full moon would be out that night and that I feel very much like climbing to the top of the gigantic mass of rocks known as Mont Salève." The next day at 9 A. M. he again wrote to Cozens but from the mountaintop: "Where do you think I am writing this from? From the summit of a lofty mountain. I gaze at an assemblage of substantial vapours which hover above, beneath, and around me... Full five hours have I waited the dissipation of the fog; but hark! A sullen rustling among the forests below... proclaims the North Wind has arisen. Look! What blasts begin to range through the atmosphere! What majesty in those volumes of gray cloud that sweep along... Mark! They are succeeded by curling volumes of blueish gray like the smoke of a declining volcano..."

The dream of Indra now seized the young student of illuminism. The day would come when the tower of Fonthill would replace Mont Salève. He had arrived at the point of "Become who thou art," which Nietzsche would take up a century later. With Beckford sensibility was also a form of snobbishness; the impossible amused him; several years were to elapse before he would realize that some passions were constraints and limitations, and lead him to become a misanthrope. For the moment he needed "to see a genius or two sometimes," and to have a secret friend to confide in.

He divulged the first of his projects to

England

Cozens. On December 25, 1777, writing from Geneva, he sent him what in reality is a draft of *Vathek*. The preliminary outline of this fantastic story reminds us of an Oriental legend. Two figures appear in it, a sage and "a woman who had... a spirit in her opal eyes, a fire which I dare not describe." This first version, written when he was seventeen, was the precursor of others, which he was not to write until he was twenty-one and which would ultimately emerge as *Vathek*.

In those four years Beckford came to understand the kind of man he was to be and the superman he wished to be. His self-instruction was "be wise," but since his meeting with Cozens he knew the course his life would take. The "be wise" was thus a kind of temporary limitation. "However irksome and discordant to the worldlings round me," he wrote, "in spite of them, I will be happy..."

It was not to be. The opinions of the worldlings mattered. It was they who would oblige him to roam abroad, far from his own land. Much later, Fonthill would be a retreat built as much to hurl disdain from the height of its towers onto his countrymen as to revive his dreams of the past.

Were those letters addressed to Cozens from Geneva read by Lettice, who accompanied Beckford to Switzerland? Or was the proximity of Voltaire, philosophers of nature, geographers, geologists, and theosophists enough

to alarm the parson? Mrs. Beckford suddenly arrived to take her son home. He was eighteen, and it was time for him to see the great houses of his own country.

On his return he went to Powderham Castle, near Exeter, home of the Courtenays, whose French, Scottish, and English branches were descended from the Emperors of Constantinople. The heir to the title, a boy of thirteen baptized William like Beckford, had a melancholy, languishing air, black curls and a faraway expression. Beckford was instantly intoxicated.

"It is a sad thing that I cannot see you every day and every hour," Beckford wrote to him on his return to Fonthill, "since you are the only person (yes let me repeat it once more) to whom I can communicate my feelings—or to whom I can disclose the strange wayward passion which throbs this very instant in my bosom."

The letter then turned into a description of a dream which had entranced Beckford on the first night of his return to his mother's home. He had had an angelic vision of the child in a "dreary cave—across which ran several bubbling streams." But how could he get the message to him?

Charlotte Courtenay, aunt of the boy whom he thereafter called Kitty, was a friend of Beckford. He made her his messenger, fascinated as she no doubt was by his charm.

In the meantime, Mrs. Beckford, concerned

at William's morbid humor, tried to entertain him. She invited William's cousins to Fonthill, Louisa Pitt and her younger sister Marcia. Louisa, imaginative, unhappily married, and consumptive, was to become the enraptured confidante of the peculiar love tormenting the young man whom she dreamed of making her lover.

But the autocratic and watchful mother (she could have served as a model for Carathis, the mother of Vathek) promptly intervened and decided that her son should travel for a year. He had to part from Kitty and Louisa from June, 1780, to April, 1781.

In Italy affairs as unconventional as those he had left behind amused him for a time. Although overwhelmed by the pontifical splendor of Rome, he noted, thinking of a friend in Venice : "I wonder no sorcerer has... offered some compact with Lucifer. I think I should have signed it with my blood, such were my desires to secure a certain object... I still sigh under an oppression for which I can hardly account."

But when he set out for London and came closer to his country, memories of Kitty consumed him. First he inquired for news of him from Louisa, then from the boy's aunt Charlotte, who was living in Paris: "Pray tell me if your nephew be as fond as ever of those ethereal amusements and if he looks forward with pleasure to the moment of my return. Of all the human creatures, male or female, with which I have been acquainted in various countries and at different periods he is the only one that seems to have been cast in my mould... I cannot understand why he has ceased answering my letters... The possibility of losing [his friendship] gives me the most cruel alarms..."

While he waited in Paris in 1781 to return to England he found some consolation with Georgina Seymour, daughter of one of Mme du Barry's lovers. But he left her and from Margate on April 14 he wrote to Cozens: "I have just landed, shaking in every nerve..."

Obstacles still stood between him and Kitty. First, Beckford's mother was reinforcing her hold on the son to whom she was bequeathing a vast fortune and for whom she had taken steps to arrange a seat in Parliament, organized receptions, and commissioned a painter—Romney. Second, Louisa, the confidante, came to London to collect the spurious fruit of so much sympathetic understanding expended in reading letters in which the only concern was for Kitty. Delectable fruit, probably, for she wrote to him: "William, my lovely infernal! How gloriously you write of iniquities... like another Lucifer..." Cunning Louisa, who knew the right words to use. Fortunately, spring, always a dangerous time for those who are consumptive, had come, and Louisa had to leave London for rest in Thuringia. She had hardly gone, when Georgina arrived. This time

England

Beckford took refuge at Fonthill and, by August, had met Kitty again at Powderham. It was a time of effusiveness, joy, stories of traveling in Italy and France, and a plan for a grand reception to reveal to the world the new squire of Fonthill. The reception took place a month later, a princely occasion which drew "above ten thousand people," neighbors, relatives, connections, possible matches (Mrs. Beckford thought of Lady Margaret Gordon, daughter of the Earl of Aboyne), and nearby villagers.

The host had three opera singers come from Italy and made them promise to return at Christmas, for another party of a very different kind was already taking shape in his mind. Cozens and Louisa discreetly went from group to group to attract the most promising talent to a Fonthill Christmas party in honor of Kitty. The young Hamilton cousins and their tutor, an Orientalist, were invited as well as the Earl of Dunmore's daughters because they were so eager to come. Others of less impeccable antecedence were also asked.

During the final weeks of 1781, the lives of Beckford and his close friends, especially Louisa and Jacques Philippe Loutherbourg, a stage designer and painter working in London for the illustrious actor David Garrick, were directed towards the triumphant Christmas party for Kitty's delectation. It would be easy to bring him to Fonthill. He was safely away from the family home and now at Westminster School in London, where Cozens and Romney, from whom Beckford had commissioned Kitty's portrait, could handle the situation.

"Let us seize the planetary hour, my beloved Louisa," wrote Beckford. "Let us enjoy uncontrolled delights before they are declared High Treason." And he "conjured" her to obtain her husband's permission to come alone to Fonthill for Christmas.

The great day approached. The Beckfords, mother and aunts, and Louisa's husband were at Bath. Fonthill was converted into a palace of the Arabian Nights... Kitty was on the way, asleep in the carriage between Cozens and Romney.

Beckford had succeeded in convincing Louisa of the splendor of his dreams. He had ordered all the decorative changes at Fonthill. The two portraits of Kitty and Beckford by Romney were hung side by side in the entrance hall, symbols of a grand passion.

Beckford was twenty-one and the master of Fonthill as he waited for the sixteen-year-old Kitty, the Courtenay heir, and Louisa, who was about his own age. The saturnalia of December 25, 26, and 27 was dedicated to Beckford's passion which lasted his entire life. It was not until he was eighty that he turned against Kitty. In the intervening years, separated from him by Kitty's family, he strove in vain to rediscover him in other people.

But what really happened at Fonthill at

Christmas, 1781? One may be certain that nothing occurred which was as "extraordinary," "demoniac," or "horrible" as the imagination of the participants and those who subsequently manufactured the "scandal" so complacently represented it.

As Beckford said of his dream palace: "It was the realization of romance in all its extravagance." Louisa was the least discreet. Two months after the event, she wrote from Bath to her Lucifer: "I am miserable at having only a little victim to prepare for sacrifice on your altar. I wish to God my William (her five-year-old son) were old enough for it. He grows every day more and more beautiful, and will in a few years answer your purpose to perfection." Later, in April, 1783, Beckford, with Kitty at his side, wrote to Louisa: "What would I not give for you to take him once more in your arms and communicate the delicious poison of your kisses..."

A triangle of love... Fifty years of Freud and of analytic fiction have unraveled some of the mystery. What first shocked English puritanism was not so much Beckford's homosexuality as Louisa's adultery. Her impenitent sinning ended in tubercular agony.

The memory of that Christmas night was too overwhelming for Beckford to forget. The effect of those few hours was permanent and remained with him day and night. A note on the fly-leaf of one of his personal copies of *Vathek* reads: "The fit I laboured under when I wrote *Vathek* lasted three days and two nights." Did Beckford really take only some sixty hours to write the work? He probably completed *Vathek* in four months, and during this time he went out a great deal. Undoubtedly the essence had been expressed in his first fitful days of work. Once completed he gave the text to Lady Craven. The next day he had to leave England, to be out of earshot of the outraged cries of his mother who was appalled by the expense of his Christmas revelries and to avoid the trap of marriage.

He embarked for the continent on May 16, 1782, with horses, carriages, beds, and baggage, accompanied by Robert Cozens, and his favorite harpsichordist, doctor, and chaplain. Lady Craven had only the time to write to him about *Vathek:* "My god what a dream! Pure Beckfordism from one end to the other, but how beautiful, how horribly beautiful." Beckford was already far away. Ostend, Cologne, Augsburg, Padua, Rome... Kitty was constantly watched by the Courtenay family and Louisa was dying. "Although I am scarcely able to hold a pen, I cannot allow anyone but myself to prepare you for an event which, in all probability, is imminent. William, I must leave you... I have sealed up your picture and letters in a packet which Marcia shall deliver into your hands after my death. Farewell, I am dying, your Louisa."

England

For a time, Louisa cheated death. From doctor to doctor and cure to cure, her life lingered on in lonely hotels, where one waits expectantly for death without ever being certain of its inevitability. She wrote often to Beckford from these retreats, often dwelling on one night of December, 1781; and her saga was her correspondence and love for Beckford. She was almost always alone, since her husband and son remained in England. William continued his travels. She was no longer his accomplice. He wrote rarely, but occasionally encouraged her with talk of future saturnalia and new Christmas nights. Ultimately she learned of his return to London to marry—at his mother's insistence—thus saving his reputation so that he could live and realize his dreams at Fonthill. Louisa strove vainly in her letters to rekindle his love, reminding him of their night at Fonthill, but it was Kitty, not Louisa, who dominated his thoughts.

"Oh William! I cannot bear to die, save me, hold me in your arms, in them I can only expire with joy," Louisa implored Beckford from Nice. He arranged by letter to meet her in Lyons. She arrived, waited twenty days, left, and died.

Meanwhile Beckford had married Lady Margaret Gordon. He had no desire for scandal and was willing to behave in a manner befitting his position, while pleasing his mother and family, who wanted him to follow a political career. Why not marry, then? Louisa was forgotten, and Courtenay was renounced. There had in fact been little fuss, and it was only because Courtenay was an added factor in the adultery that Beckford had written to Louisa: "Each day I fall lower in everyone's opinion."

After Louisa's death and his marriage to Lady Margaret, Satan's star ascended. Soon the husband was a father and a member of the Lower House of Parliament with the peerage only a short step away and, thanks to his mother's intrigues, a barony would soon be his... What? Him? A voluptuary, a homosexual, an atheist, a man of wealth and taste! A liberal, too. What more need be said!

But wait! As he himself wrote (but too late), he was about to be "trapped" and "humiliated." It could not be said that an individual "who, regardless of Divine, Natural and Human Law," sinks "below the lowest class of brutes in the most preposterous rites" (thus declaimed the *Morning Herald*) is more powerful than an eminent judge, Lord Longhborough, Solicitor General and Chief Justice of the Common Pleas. Lord Longhborough had married Charlotte Courtenay, Kitty's aunt, who had acted as Beckford's messenger. Her husband was now the *éminence grise* of Powderham, the Courtenay home.

Summer had arrived and Beckford's wife was pregnant. They went to Fonthill to enjoy the country air. What did they find on arrival?

An invitation from Lord Courtenay, asking William and his wife to spend the end of the summer at Powderham. Beckford had not seen Kitty since his marriage. Obviously his forthcoming elevation to the peerage... What should they do? Lady Beckford had one of those intuitions which only mothers have and advised him not to go, but her son disregarded her.

At Powderham the welcome was friendly. Only Kitty seemed bothered, perhaps because of the presence of Lady Margaret. Beckford soon forgot that he was there with his pregnant wife and with all his social prestige nearly, if not completely, reestablished. He calmly undertook to spend three weeks near the boy whom he adulated. However blind he may have been, he did at least realize that Kitty avoided him. The inevitable, of course, occurred. One October evening, determined to discover the truth, Beckford entered Kitty's room and bolted the door. Firing questions in his penetrating voice, he awaited Kitty's whispered, melancholy reply. Instead, he heard sharp knocks on the door.

The ambush had succeeded. The entire household was present—the father, aunt, wife, servants, and the Chief Justice himself—and utterly outraged.

At dawn on October 13 the Beckfords started back to Fonthill, and Beckford wrote to his friend the Reverend Samuel Henley about his experience: "Oh! How I was trapped and humiliated."

The scandal was out. The gossips got what they wanted. The *Morning Herald* demanded names. The *Public Advisor* announced the departure of "this man who was about to become an English peer," adding that he left in the company of Kitty.

But Beckford refused to go. He resisted his mother, Margaret's brother who sought a duel, and Margaret's family. The most he would consent to do was to shut himself up alone at Fonthill.

Self-righteous keepers of the public conscience know well the value of delving into their intended victim's past. Christmas, 1781... Necromancers... Switzerland... Italy... Such goings on! Worse still, Kitty, reputedly whipped, signed confessions and gave them to Longhborough, the Chief Justice and his uncle.

In April, 1785, Beckford consented to leave England with his wife, who had just borne him a daughter. Exile on the continent. The birth of a second daughter in Geneva found him a widower. He missed his wife sufficiently to feel a measure of distress and to record it. This did not prevent him from being suspected by some as her killer.

There was thus no place for Beckford in English society, but the Latin world remained. Before leaving Geneva, he made a pilgrimage to Mont Salève in search of childhood memories. His first concern was to establish the whereabouts of his copy of *Vathek*. He wrote to

England

London, only to learn that the book had already been published in a translation by Henley entitled *The History of the Caliph Vathek: An Arabian Tale from an Unpublished Manuscript with Critical Notes and Analysis.* Henley claimed authorship, but proceedings were pointless, for he had absconded with the original French manuscript. There was nothing for Beckford to do but rewrite the work from Henley's English translation. *Vathek* was finally published in Lausanne, and Beckford was free to leave for Paris where he found what he adored— the heady incense of intrigue. Everything was for sale in the Paris of 1784. Beckford was introduced by the architect Claude Nicolas Ledoux to a magician in a mysterious Armide pavilion deep in the plain of Villeneuve-Saint-Georges. The mystery of occult meetings made him forget that Paris, not far from Revolution, was no longer the haunt of frivolity. He stayed long enough to promise himself a return visit. After leaving instructions with his buyers to acquire antiques in his absence, he secretly returned to London. But the "Queen-Mother" and her adviser, appalled at the risk he was taking, sent him off posthaste to Jamaica.

Beckford embarked on the *Julius Caesar.* The vessel was attacked by Barbary pirates and he narrowly escaped capture. The thought of being sold in Africa persuaded him to stay on land and to make his way to Lisbon, where he found a cultivated society prepared to accept him. A British ambassador, clearly acting on instructions, prevented him from meeting the royal family, however.

This annoyance was temporarily mitigated by the beauty of Catholic ritual and religious ceremonies. Beckford spent his days in prayer, or rather in ecstasy. The music, the choirs, the vestments, and the soaring Gothic vaulting offered him a foretaste of what Fonthill might be. The clergy were on his side, although they knew quite well who he was. His presence day and night at mass evoked in their eyes the image of a prodigal son. Besides, he was as generous as a lord. At times Beckford thought of settling in Portugal. With a few sheep in a meadow, he could very well imagine himself at Fonthill.

Time was passing, and Beckford had still not been received by the king and queen. This inequity led him to loathe Portugal and all Englishmen in the person of their ambassador. Were he to return to London he would court trouble from Longhborough, who had his letters to Kitty. His family also implored him to keep away. "When will I stop playing the part of the wandering Jew and no longer be stared at as if I bore the mark of divine malediction?"

There were compensations, however. His vivid account of an excursion to the monasteries of Batalha and Alcobaça reads like an imaginary journal. But diversions did little to disguise the fact that, although he was the son of a

Hamilton and a Lord Mayor of London, the long arm of English etiquette and moral protocol reached as far as Lisbon. The "black sheep" of London was as "black" as ever to influential circles on the European continent. He decided to go to Spain and in Madrid was received by the royal family. For the second time in his life, he became the lover of a married woman, the older Marquesa of Santa Cruz, who proposed that they elope to Portugal because of her fear of gossip. Dismayed at the suggestion, he packed his bags to leave for Paris, but not so hurriedly as to forget the paintings of Velásquez and Murillo which he had bought in Spain for Fonthill.

In France the Revolution was simmering. Arriving in Paris during the summer of 1788, he installed himself in the Hôtel d'Orsay, Rue de Varenne, with his Spanish dwarf (of French origin), Pierre de Graichy, and Gregorio Franchi, a Portuguese seminarist who rendered to perfection the glorious compositions of Haydn and who became his secretary. He does not seem to have been concerned about the September convocation of the Estates General. Lord Courtenay died in England, and his letters to Kitty were no longer likely to be used against him. Beckford decided to return to London. He left orders with agents and dealers to buy everything of interest that turned up during his absence.

In London he told Elizabeth Craven: "I am growing rich and am preparing to build towers." He had already thrown down a challenge in *Vathek* for a tower of fifteen hundred stairs, from which "men looked like ants and hills like molehills." His was an ambitious project. He determined to rebuild Fonthill Abbey as quickly as possible in order to squelch the nobles of Wiltshire who still thought him a black sheep. "When my hills are completely blackened with fir, I shall retreat into the centre of this gloomy circle... There will I build my tower and lock myself up with my books and writings to brood over them until Heaven closes my eyes on this strange medley of malevolent beings..."

Beckford had become an anglophobe and dreamed of surrounding Fonthill with a great wall of China. He asked James Wyatt, who had been engaged to restore Windsor Castle and was a proponent of the Gothic Revival style, to prepare a design for his Fonthill retreat. Wyatt wanted to create an artificial ruin or a "castle" in the style of Horace Walpole's "gimcrack villa" at Strawberry Hill, but Beckford wanted a tower of 280 feet, higher than that of Westminster. The project was stillborn. As soon as Beckford and the architect had reached agreement, Wyatt was called to work on the royal palace, and the king had to come first.

Beckford, in November, 1791, left for Paris. He undoubtedly derived a perverse pleasure,

England

as a member of the English liberal aristocracy, in making the trip to the continent while French nobles were making the same journey in the opposite direction to England. He was certain that his journey would be an unusual experience, first because, as the son of a Lord Mayor who had defied a king, his name was known to the Revolutionaries. Second, as an avid collector, he felt obliged to be where furniture and other pieces were being sold at phenomenally low prices. Third, the Revolution was an experience to be lived like that solitary night on Mont Salève.

His life in Paris was pure Beckfordism. Thanks to his origins, the dandy won the esteem of the Revolutionaries. He was admired for being rich, blue-blooded, and anti-royalist at the same time. Of him everything was permitted. He could be charming when circumstances required, and the uneasy aspect of events and relationship between the Revolutionaries appealed to him. Moreover, he felt aloof from the conflict, although it certainly entertained him, just as religious splendor, dwarfs, and those legendary Fonthill revelries had stimulated his instinctive susceptibility to the unusual.

The Revolutionaries immediately helped him to set up in one of the handsome town houses on the Rue de Grenelle, and allotted him the loge of the Prince de Condé at the Opéra. He no longer felt compelled to meet one or two geniuses a week, for now he was satisfied to meet and entertain nobles and Revolutionaries in turn. He was especially attracted by the dissident factions within the Revolutionary movement itself. In 1791 he claimed to be an anarchist, explaining that: "I care not whether they are aristocrats or democrats! I am an autocrat determined to make the best of every situation."

And Fonthill? He wrote to his steward to economize as much as he might think proper. He had forgotten Fonthill and everyone and everything in England.

He bought all he could in the way of signed furniture, statues, and china, commissioned the royal cabinetmakers, and went regularly to see the bookseller Chardin, who was instructed to find him the rarest copies and choicest bindings. His 500,000 pound income from the sugar and spice trade in Jamaica gave him a free hand in France. But England's entry into war with France in February, 1793, forced him to return to London. He wanted to disregard it, but Wildman, his steward, tried to make him understand that he would either be an enemy alien in France or a traitor to England. The only effect of this advice was to make him burn all papers revealing his relations with the Revolutionaries, for no traces of diaries or records have ever been found, and it seems improbable that he had none.

Apparently, Beckford obtained more than

books from the booksellers and perhaps because of them he remained undiscovered, for he was living at this time under the protection of Mérigot le Jeune in the guise of a bookseller's clerk, after having been in Savoy for a summer visit and carrying off some of the musical instruments of the Royal Guard. During the September massacres he was on Lake Geneva at Evian and would have liked to enter Switzerland, but Geneva was closed to him since his wife's death. He returned to Paris in the middle of the Terror. We shall never know whether he was present when Louis XVI was beheaded, as has been supposed. We do know, however, that he arranged for Chardin, his bookseller, to receive an income for life of 2,400 francs. We shall never know if he met the Marquis de Sade, at that time secretary of the *Section des Piques,* or whether Marat protected him. We do know that, three months before Marat's assassination, Beckford succeeded in getting back to London in May, 1793, with a passport from the Commune, when it was almost impossible for any foreigner to leave France. He had tried before in April, but the livery of one of his servants had given him away. He now succeeded within ten days, thanks to the Revolutionary Committee of the Commune, in obtaining his permit in the name of W. Beckford, "foreigner whose departure Paris sees with regret."

Beckford arrived in London with the finest Boulle furniture from Versailles and a number of objects for Fonthill which can now be seen in the Louvre, the British Museum and the Metropolitan Museum. The "new" Fonthill was still not built. Beckford decided to return to Lisbon, where in 1795 he was at last received by the Regent and presented at court without the approval of the British ambassador and in utter disregard of protocol. During his travels he visited Montserrat, where fourteen years later (1809) Byron was to retrace his path before writing *Childe Harold:*

There thou too, Vathek! England's wealthiest son,
Once formed thy paradise...
Here didst thou dwell, here schemes of pleasure plan
Beneath yon mountain's ever beauteous brow;
But now, as if a thing unblest by man,
Thy fairy dwelling is as lone as thou!

(*Childe Harold,* I)

The walls of Montserrat, admired by Byron, were not Beckford's idea of architecture. "Me, build that!" he is supposed to have exclaimed one day when reading *Childe Harold.* "It was the work of a Falmouth carpenter."

Beckford soon felt that he had had enough of Portugal. He embarked for Naples, was nearly captured and returned to Madrid. In 1796 he returned to Fonthill with plans for his future home.

129

England

At thirty-six Beckford had few ambitions beyond his solitary retreat. During this comparatively early period he conceived his designs for an octagon, which would form the axis of the future abbey, and from which would radiate cloisters and galleries. If *Vathek* had been written by Beckford in adolescence, the abbey of Fonthill was constructed by a Beckford in full maturity, disdainful of hunts and the traditions of the aloof and narcissistic English gentry. "If the honour and esteem of my country are to be earned only by conformity to such idle modes as these, I must do without them; besides, the scythe of the Revolution relentlessly pursues its course."

Work at Fonthill never progressed quickly enough for the taste of Beckford since Wyatt was more a planner than a realizer. The structure began to take shape in 1797, but Beckford was not able to install himself in his abbey, with its furnished galleries hung with red and gold velvet, until 1807. The octagon, whose arches rose nearly one hundred feet, was illuminated by four stained-glass windows. The Saint Michael gallery housed a library, as large as that of the Vatican, with an abbé in charge. Beckford's collections of furniture and artifacts were distributed throughout the rooms and corridors, together with his paintings by Breughel, Veronese, Rembrandt, Van Eyck, and Raphael. There were more than sixty fireplaces. The bedrooms and windows were trouble-somely narrow. Beckford chose a simple monk's cell as his bedroom and slept on a low bed.

The former château, scene of the revels of 1781, had been demolished. The tower built as a replacement was guarded by the dwarf Perro dressed in golden livery. Beckford's secretary, Gregorio Franchi, reputedly organized debaucheries, and no woman, it was alleged, was allowed in Beckford's presence.

The abbey was in fact a tomb as Beckford admitted: "The world and society surrounding me are as cold as a tomb: the pale Ambroise, the infamous Poupée, the horrible Goule, the insipid Mme Bion, the cadaverous Nicolus, the solemn dwarf, the frigid silence and Salisbury plain..." There were still two radiant figures at Fonthill, each in his own particular way, the dwarf janitor and, a frequent visitor, the painter Turner. There were other minor satellites: Benjamin West, the American painter; Clarke, the London bookseller; and Abbé Macquin, an elderly French archivist and unfrocked priest, known as a gourmand and toper.

Beckford was no longer interested in diversions. What, then, were his interests? He had had his share of love, exile, and greatness. Blasé? No; at the age of eighty he asserted that he still wanted life, but that life no longer wanted him. Misanthropic? Yes... He successfully married his daughter Susan to the future Duke of Hamilton after four years of financial negotiation, necessitated by the demanding duke. Nobody came to the ceremony, but Susan Beckford did become a Hamilton. The second daughter, who had fallen into less ambitious love with a far from wealthy colonel, became *l'infâme ordure* and was disinherited. All that was left to him was his platoon of servants—Bijou (Jewel), Miss Long, the Comtesse Vérole (Pox), the Comtesse Papillon (Butterfly), whose nicknames reflected the disgust Beckford felt. "We will need different angels, if we are to enter another paradise," he wrote to Franchi.

Catching sight of a tightrope walker one evening at the Royal Circus revived his dreams, and Beckford felt compelled to bring him back to Fonthill. "I fear that the angel is no longer at the circus... Oh! What a blessed creature... What happiness to save such a beautiful soul." All Beckford's men pursued the vanished angel, but in vain. The price of Jamaican sugar dropped. He had to sell his horses, paintings, and ultimately Fonthill. The tightrope walker danced in his dreams, just as Kitty had done in the past.

"For the love of God, do all you can to find this final charm able to free me from this melancholic nothingness..."

Work on the abbey proceeded at intervals, despite Beckford's financial troubles and the "sublime" Wyatt's lackadaisical supervision. "Some people," Beckford said, "drink to forget their misfortunes; I have stopped drinking to build and so doing insure my ruin... *Edificabo ecclesiam meam.*"

Beckford's towers were a Biblical challenge to the world. The tone of his letters had now become apocalyptic: "A structure as grand as Fonthill Abbey evokes national ruin... How difficult it is to find salvation! The only accessible path I have to follow leads to Satan..."

Beckford in his writing opened his path to Byron, Baudelaire, and Poe, who recognized him as a fraternal soul. His wealth did not stifle his genius and impassioned life, because ultimately the love of one being drew him into a passion for follies.

Beckford the ruined prince was as great as Beckford the builder and visionary. He attached no importance to the loss of a part of his collection and all of his towers. The waning of his life forces was more distracting than material events and architectural fantasies which were ultimately outside the realm of his romantic passions.

On June 25, 1809, while changing horses at an inn, Byron heard that two other carriages were on the same road that day, one occupied by Beckford and the other by Lord Courtenay, the young Kitty.

Byron had tried in vain to persuade Beckford to receive him at Fonthill, for Beckford had little liking for his admirer and disciple and felt no obligation to wait upon him. When Byron learned that Beckford was to spend that

England

night at the posting-house, he hoped to catch a glimpse of him, but dared not violate Beckford's privacy. Byron wrote that Courtenay's costume and makeup were surpassed only by Beckford's appearance.

Some years later Fonthill was sold to a gunpowder dealer; three years after the sale the tower collapsed.

Beckford retired to Bath to live in two cottages owned by his mother and her sisters. There he installed the best items of his surviving collection. His optimism was genuine. "He had no wish for a literary reputation," wrote Samuel Rogers. Beckford confided to his doctor, Schöll of Lausanne, that "for twenty years I have never been so rich, so independent, and so tranquil... I have considerable means and no debts." He laughed at the collapse of Wyatt's tower, suggesting that its new owner would sell the remains stone by stone in the neighborhood. "I could live another hundred years until I lose my good health; and, at present there is no reason to think otherwise." The *Episodes*, which he wrote as a sequel to *Vathek* and the tales of the *Hall of Eblis*, which Byron would have so much liked to hear Beckford read, were personal property and would not be published, unless the publisher were to "persuade himself, and feel inspired to offer a sum as round as the great globe itself..."

Henceforth, Fonthill was his "unpublished" work. He had no need for others... no need to build towers or buy the furniture of kings, or pay society the required price for a proper reputation. He even went so far as to ignore critics and admirers alike. Byron was not received by Beckford. Shelley fared no better, for Beckford had no sympathy for that young "Satanic School" and its nineteenth-century protagonists. He had paid too high a price for the right to be respected and had no further taste for what went on about him. Even if he had been an incubator for the fledglings of the period, he remained unaware of them, just as Chateaubriand was unaware of the dreams which he had inspired and of what they might become. Perhaps one man among the younger generation interested him, Benjamin Disraeli, a "man with the finest taste. What mad originality! What poetic intensity!" Beckford still went for long rides on his thoroughbred gray, led by his dwarf, surrounded by a pack of hounds and liveried grooms and looking like an apparition from hell to the townspeople of Bath. As he lay dying from a chill, caught in the rain on one such excursion, he refused a parson, but agreed to see his granddaughter, Lady Lincoln. He died on a low and narrow campbed. He had provoked society out of pure passion, seldom deliberately. Society had condemned him to exile and then accepted him as a wealthy recluse. He died indifferent to himself, his passions, his conceits, and the rest of the world.

102. *Fonthill Abbey painted by William Turner. The artist was one of the few men whose company Beckford enjoyed during his declining years.*

102

103

104

◁ 103. *William Beckford, the Satanic prince, painted by*
George Romney in 1781. A portrait of Lord Courtenay was
also done by Romney. The two paintings faced each other at
Fonthill.

106. *Architectural drawing of the cross section of the main*
gallery. The gallery was illuminated by heraldic stained-glass
windows. The building was one of the first examples of the
return to the Gothic style. The main salon contained a neo-
Gothic fireplace and Regency furniture.
▽

105. *View of Fonthill about 1800.* ▽

105

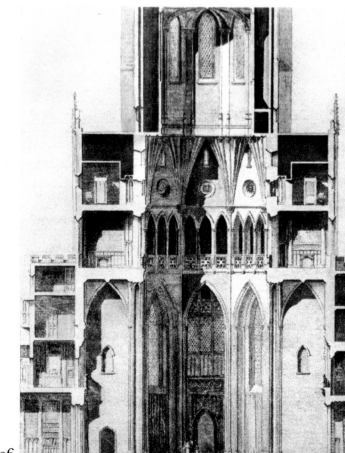

106

107

108

109

107-114. *Furniture once in Fonthill Abbey. Despite the risk to his life, Beckford stayed in Paris during the reign of Terror to acquire these royal pieces.*

110

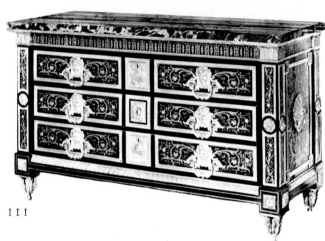

111

◁ 110. *Louis XVI commode by J. H. Riesener. Oak, lacquer, and bronze. Metropolitan Museum of Art, New York.*

◁ 111. *Louis XVI commode by Étienne Levasseur. Shell and brass.*

114. *Wardrobe by Boulle. Shell and brass. Louvre, Paris.* ▽

112

◁ 112. *Louis XVI escritoire by J. H. Riesener. Ebony, lacquer, and gilt bronze. Metropolitan Museum of Art, New York.*

113. *Louis XVI desk by J. B. Leclerc. Oak and bronze. Beckford's desk is now in the Condé Museum in Chantilly.* ▽

113

114

The Castle of Ambras

For Ferdinand II, Archduke of Austria, a castle with a gallery of portraits of freaks and pictures of strange animals, a room with armor for giants and dwarfs, and thirty-eight showcases for the wonders of nature and rare objects.

Ambras, perched like an eagle's nest above Innsbruck, Austria, is probably the castle which has best preserved the spirit of the unusual so eagerly cultivated in the sixteenth century by the nobility in Bavaria and Prussia. The princes of the House of Hapsburg lived on the borders of Hungary, Czechoslovakia, and Russia. One, the creator of Ambras, was Ferdinand II, Archduke of Austria and Regent of Tyrol. He was probably influenced by both Rome and the Russian steppes, borrowing from the former a taste for painting, sculpture, and furniture and from the latter a predilection for magic items and freaks of nature—peculiar animals, rare stones, and the unexpected meeting and fusion of the animal and plant world into a single object. An example of the last may be seen in the Ambras collection in one item which looks like branches sprouting from a tree trunk but is in reality the antlers of a stag. The animal died at the foot of a tree which gradually assimilated the antlers over a period of time.

At Ambras, Ferdinand II was the model of an enthusiastic collector, whose passion surpassed his resources but whose curiosity compensated for his lack of money. This curiosity gives Ambras its unity. Its collections are noted for their rarity rather than their commercial value. Some of the collections, including the armor, were valuable enough to attract Napoleon. He transferred the finest pieces, including Emperor Maximilian's armor, to the Belvédère in Vienna in 1814.

Today, most of Ferdinand II's collections, sold by his son after his death to the Emperor Rudolph, have been returned to their original site in Ambras. The nature of the objects displayed and the manner in which they are arranged give us an idea of what a sixteenth-century cabinet of curios was like. The only other insight into such curio cabinets is provided by contemporary engravings which show large rooms furnished with wardrobes or chests of drawers containing such strange objects as shells, minerals, precious stones, coins, stuffed birds and animals, and dried fish, all of which are displayed as mannerist still lifes.

Ferdinand II's youth, perhaps, explains his need for such unusual collections. Although the nephew of Emperor Charles V and the

137

115. *Ferdinand II, Regent of Tyrol, was a collector of unusual objects. To satisfy his follies, he never had more than the comparatively limited wealth of an archduke at his disposal.*

younger brother of Emperor Maximilian I, he was reared in the country by his mother outside the active life of brilliant court society. The grand figures of his family gave Ferdinand neither political responsibilities nor the means with which to equal their magnificent receptions. Ferdinand received the education of a Hapsburg, but, as a younger son, he was not awarded the fortune to match it. His whole life was oriented toward acquiring the objects which he coveted as best he could with the means he had available.

For this reason, the life of the Regent of Tyrol was devoted to seeking rare natural items and objects rather than acquiring objects on the expensive European art market. When it became fashionable to collect armor, he resorted to cunning and diplomacy. He wrote to all the emperors and princes whom he considered important and worthy of being represented at Ambras, and invited them to offer him one of their own suits of armor for his great hall. They were also asked to provide a portrait and biography. This would ensure them a place among other, often more important, persons of rank, a list of whom he attached to his letter. This method of collecting may seem rather shocking, but it amused and pleased the recipients of Ferdinand's letters. Moreover, the fame of the donors added value to the gifts presented. The armor of princes and kings, accompanied by biographical notes, was placed next to the armor of Ferdinand's jesters, giants, and dwarfs.

As did Peter the Great of Russia many years later in his palace in Saint Petersburg, Ferdinand surrounded himself at Ambras with a staff of giants or dwarfs. During his life, Peter the Great had included in his collection of freaks the skeleton of his valet, who was over six feet nine inches tall and had died in his service. He had also preserved the valet's heart in a jar of formaldehyde, which can still be seen in the Leningrad Folk Museum. Such a penchant for extremes was supposed to reveal a special disposition for understanding.

Both Ferdinand and Peter the Great would have probably been more interested in a white stag with five hooves than in a bronze sculpture by Cellini or a painting by Veronese. This may be the reason that Ferdinand's collection, forgotten for so long, arouses interest today as a reflection of the search for an absolute through unusual objects.

To house his collections, Ferdinand II had a second castle built under the residential castle—the real residence complemented by a dream residence. The latter contained so many objects that one man would not have sufficed to collect them, had he not been aided by researchers, procurers, travelers, secretaries, and connoisseurs.

The second house was mainly occupied by the collection of arms and armor; ivory and ebony cabinets, whose drawers contained gems and precious stones; furniture inlaid with marble still lifes crowned by ivory statuettes, towers of Babel, spiral staircases and pyramids of gilded wood. Different colored cabinets contained various objects. The first, blue, held more than thirty varieties of rock-crystal; the second, green, silverware; the third, red, hard rocks; the fourth, white, musical instruments; the fifth, automatons, astronomical instruments and pendulums; the sixth and seventh, objects made of stone and marble; the eighth, books; the ninth, artifacts made of birds' feathers. The nine other cabinets—there were eighteen in all—contained items made of alabaster, blown and engraved glass, coral, and porcelain. To this should be added stuffed lizards and sharks hung from the ceiling, and, on the walls, pictures of real animals, whose curious dress and unusual number of legs or horns belonged to the domain of unreality. The collections of Ambras lacked only the mythical unicorn, represented perhaps by the tusk of a narwhal.

The white cabinets of Ambras still contain crystals and objects carved from crystal such as cups, candlesticks, and goblets in the form of birds and peacocks. The old green cabinets still have their Augsburg silver, often decorated with lapis lazuli and coral. The automatons and pendulums of the fifth cabinet still exist along with items made of hard stone and Italian marble tables decorated with scenes

from mythology or the Crucifixion made of inlaid and carved coral.

Nature inspired and guided the imagination of Ferdinand II, who chose the subjects to be treated according to the material brought to him. He liked mother-of-pearl and collected small boxes, goblets, and dishes of this substance, generally made in Florence but occasionally copied in Tyrol and Austria. There was also a collection of bezoars, magic objects of a period in which intellectual enlightenment was accompanied by the most pagan superstitions. Bezoars, concretions found in the stomachs of camels, are the rarest items at Ambras. One bezoar, mounted by Ferdinand in gold, looks like a golden apple of the Hesperides, and was thought to be a precious talisman capable of altering the destiny of anyone using it. Also in the collection are hollow sculpted rhinoceros horns, said to be an antidote for poison—wine containing arsenic, drunk from a cup shaped from the tusks of one of these animals, had no effect on an intended victim.

Three centuries later, magic was no longer a subject of speculation for princes, and Napoleon had to order his silversmiths to make salt and pepper shakers which could be locked to prevent poison from being mixed with the condiments. Ferdinand II would have thought that all he really needed was a talisman.

Objects made of ivory and other materials called "objects of virtue," and the sorcerers' mirrors of Ambras were quite different from the purely magic items mentioned above. Although their power cannot influence fate, it works on the imagination of those who look at them. The multiple, convex image of oneself, reflected in the sorcerers' mirrors, momentarily distracts one's train of thought. The idea of lost time suggested by the "objects of virtue," which contain carved forms within forms, is also hallucinatory.

Ferdinand II, above all, expected an object of art to be associated with mystery. This explains among his collections the many curious paintings of wild men and women offered to him by his nephew, the Duke of Bavaria, who knew his tastes. These portraits, when presented, were sometimes accompanied by the artists' models. One was a bearded female dwarf who in real life married a man whose face was covered with hair. His portrait also adorned the castle's walls. She is said to have given birth to a little girl with the head of an animal.

In love, Ferdinand II showed the same independence as in his other tastes. Expected to espouse a Stuart, he secretly married Philippina Welser, a woman of the middle class, who shared his enthusiasm for collecting. While she was his mistress, they had two sons, whom he had left on the doorstep of Ambras, so that he could pretend to find them and thus be able to adopt them officially. Philippina abetted him in all his whims and kept open house. Nine hundred pounds of meat were consumed every day at Ambras (enough for two packs of two hundred hounds), and the meals had at least twenty-four courses. Philippina is said to have died of indigestion. At the age of fifty, Ferdinand married a girl of fifteen, hoping that she would give him a son. She bore him three daughters, and he left her to her devotions and spent all of his time on his collections.

116. *The façade with* trompe-l'œil *decoration of the inner courtyard of the castle. The frescoes symbolize themes associated with the cult of Dionysus. Dionysus is life. Accompanied by maenads, nymphs, satyrs, and Bacchus, he pursues pleasure to the point of its inevitable negation and end, which is death.* "Vincit potentia Forti." *Ferdinand II died in this castle, which evokes Ali Baba's cave and may be thought of as an ethnological museum of the sixteenth century.*

116

118. *Three brothers of the House of Austria: Maximilian, Ferdinand II, and Johan.*

119. *Dürer's portrait of the Emperor Maximilian, brother of Ferdinand II. Maximilian was a model of the Renaissance prince for his less wealthy brother.*

120. *The trophy room, where Ferdinand gave sumptuous feasts.*

◁ 117. *Ferdinand's chess set.*

122. *Austrian objects of virtue made of ivory, carved wood, and glass.*

121

121. *Sixteenth-century Italian and Austrian objects of ivory and mother-of-pearl. On the wall is a sorcerer's mirror.*

123. *This painting of a monkey child wearing a court robe was the present of a nobleman who knew Ferdinand's passion for freaks. The child was supposed to have lived at Ambras.*

123

124. *A gilt bronze clock. Turkish figures chime the hours. The movement of their eyes and mouths marks the seconds.*

124

125

125. *Painting of a bearded woman.*

127

Preceding page:
126. *Various objects at Ambras. A sixteenth-century coffer with drawers. Marble marquetry depicting fruits. On the right, an egg mounted on a silver figure and a medallion chest with drawers. On the left, two small boxes of gold and silver, one of which is covered with coral. The paintings depict men who lived at Ambras. The lord in the middle survived a combat in which a lance pierced his eye; he merely sawed off both ends of the lance to lessen its weight. An emir is among these men who amused an Austrian prince with a court of human freaks and stuffed animals.*

◁ 127. *Armor collection.*

128. *In one of the rooms at Ambras, armor and clothes of a giant and dwarfs belonging to Ferdinand II.* ▽

128

130. *This "child of love," son of Ferdinand II and his mistress Philippina (who later became his wife), swore to maintain the Ambras collection but sold it soon after his father died.*

Preceding page:
129. *A ceiling with the signs of the zodiac above an astonishing collection of armor.*

131. *Three portrait paintings. On the left, a dwarf and a giant belonging to Ferdinand II. On the right, two more giants from Ambras.*

Next page:
132. *Ferdinand collected the wonders of nature. A shark is suspended from the ceiling. In the showcase, a collection of coral and sculptures made of coral. In the foreground, the antlers of a deer embedded in a tree.*

133

134

133. *A Passion scene set in rock work. The impenitent thief and Christ on the cross, sculptured in coral.*

134. *Detail of a showcase of works in coral.*

135

135. *Unusal objects at Ambras. On the right, stone and ivory objects of virtue. In the foreground, set in gold and in the form of an apple, a bezoar—a rare concretion found in the stomach of a camel. On the left, a concretion mounted into a silver cup. In the background, a carved rhinoceros horn serves as a goblet.*

The Castle of Hellbrunn

The creation of a sixteenth-century archbishop, a palace with fabulous gardens containing fantastic grottoes.

In the sixteenth century Markus Sittikus, an archbishop, resided in the small Austrian town of Hellbrunn. A descendant of a noble Salzburg family, the Hohenemsers, and an ambitious man interested in the novelties of his day, he decided to advance his career by charming his emperor, Maximilian I. He erected a fantastic palace adorned with exotic gardens.

The feeling of a dream world is induced by a statue of a unicorn in the entrance hall to the castle. A sense of the exotic continues on the elaborate marble staircase, and culminates in the state apartments in a collection of paintings depicting fantastic subjects. The first represents a huge black horse, held by a Turkish servant, with eight legs and eight hooves shod in gold. An inscription authenticates the existence of this unlikely stallion, which once belonged to the archbishop's stables. Another painting shows a number of paired white animals hunting.

One of the three doors on the landing leads into the waiting room. This opens onto a chinoiserie room, which precedes the dining room in which is a large faience lighthouse made in 1608 by the Salzburg porcelain works. This is decorated with blue hunting scenes and

scenes of ancient times and the early Christian era.

A gallery extends the whole length of the castle and is painted in *trompe-l'œil* in the Florentine manner by Arsenio Mascagni. It looks like an Italian street flanked with arcades, pilasters, and mannerist figures.

The Octagonal Hall, the main room at Hellbrunn, opens on one side to the garden, and on the other to the gallery. It is also painted entirely in *trompe-l'œil*, and creates the illusion of a temple with columns flanked by female allegories. This room is crowned by a sky blue ceiling with small windows in which eagles and other birds, reflected by the checkered pattern of the marble floor, are clearly visible.

The other rooms are plain but in each are paintings of animals. Sawfish are depicted in rectangular frames the size of a dish used in serving. Other pictures are of giant vultures, unknown birds, and wild duck in the manner of watercolor illustrations from old naturalist books. The spaces above doors are adorned with depictions of stags at bay in the style of Dürer. Life and death are intimately linked in these hunting trophies. These are not works intended merely to please but rather to surprise because each of these strange creatures must

136. *The Grotto of Orpheus at the castle of Hellbrunn exemplifies the pagan and mythological world of Archbishop Markus Sittikus.*

have struck fear into the hunter's heart before being killed and painted. These paintings of beasts of prey are filled with a message, that found in Dürer's work and reminding man that death, although disguised, is always present. These are not the splendid, colorful beasts of a paradise lost as found in Italian and Flemish paintings, in Snyders, for instance, but rather specters of forests closed and alien to man.

A spiral staircase leads through the Grotto of Neptune to the garden, and offers an initial contact with an artificially contrived nature consisting of countless objects. The grottoes, fountains, and sculpture at Hellbrunn are essentially the stuff of dreams.

In the Grotto of Neptune, the god dominates everything, towering over the winged horses of a fountain above the curious mask of a man with the ears of a bat and rolling eyes and tongue. This god of the Germanic forests is found with similar traits among the popular arts of the Shamanist tribes of Siberia, as though the forest beginning in Asia and covering Europe as far as France bequeathed its residents similar divinities despite national borders. Neptune and his marble horses may disappear suddenly behind a screen of water from countless fountains spouting from the walls of the grotto. If at such a moment one happens to be in a lateral cave or inside the main grotto, it is impossible to get out without being drenched, and if one is outside, one

cannot enter. Everything seems to depend on a magician who may or may not allow one to pass, but who turns out to be only a master of water hidden behind the entrance, where he controls the mechanism of the fountains.

Leaving this grotto by the large door bordered with gigantic statues of neo-Egyptian goddesses, one is again caught under a shower of water projected from the heads of two stone stags. Springing to life, the jets shoot from their antlers and nostrils. If one tries to escape toward the balcony opposite the grotto, a screen of water hiding the stairs bars the way.

The Courtyard of Bacchus and the theater, on the right, are outside the grotto, preceded by fountains. At the center of the open-air theater is the statue of an emperor surmounted by the heraldic animals of Hellbrunn, a lion and a goat bearing the arms of Sittikus. On a pediment with allegorical figures are victorious Rome and Justitia, a throne with sculptures dating from 1616, and figures of bearded men in Oriental dress, an assemblage of incongruous objects representing sixteenth-century taste.

Guests at one time sat facing the theater at the "prince's table." This long, white marble table surrounded with benches has a groove cut into the marble top and was designed to become a fountain carrying streams of water to the four goats still adorning the table. The benches, which have holes in the center, suddenly spray water in all directions transforming the table into a quadrilateral jet of water projected high into the air.

On the other side of a bridge is the Grotto of Orpheus. Orpheus is singing to Eurydice lying at his feet and wearing a portrait of the archbishop around her neck. Sculpted animals emerge from the walls of the grotto, lured by Orpheus' song. Nothing, however, can be heard except the noise made by the water of a fountain spouting from the mouth of a sculpted goat.

The River of the Gods is crossed by a bridge lined with Tritons and built across fountains and statues of goddesses who seem to rise from the water.

After the Grotto of Shells, the Grotto of Ruins at the northwest angle of the castle simulates a grotto with fissures caused by earthquakes.

The two most enchanting grottoes, to the right of the Grotto of Neptune, are the Grotto of Mirrors and the Grotto of Birds. The former is a waiting room of blue frescoes and sorcerers' mirrors. In the second, darkness reigns enveloped in the perfume of a forest and the song of birds. Once the eyes have grown accustomed to the dark, one can observe that the blocks of rock which form the vault are covered with freshly cut branches of fir trees. The song of birds seems to come from these branches but is, in fact, produced by a water organ, the many pipes of which are operated by the natural spring on which Hell-brunn is built. This simple system has been used for four centuries. When the mechanism is working, the air escapes through the water producing chirping sounds quite similar to the song of birds. At the back of the grotto, a waterwheel draws mythological figurines associated with the water across its surface.

Leaving these grottoes and again passing through the Grotto of Neptune, we see in the axis of the latter the Bridge of the Star, and in the garden associated with this star, the statues of the four seasons. Further in the park are four small grottoes containing automatons which were described in print in 1619—the Grinder, the Martyrdom of Marsyas, the Miller, Perseus and Andromeda, and the Potter. In another grotto is a draped Venus sculpted by Johann Waldburger in 1613.

On this side of the park, the strangest surprise is the water-bell, under which can be seen a fresh flower, preserved there for months by the convex and transparent vault of water enveloping it. Further on are two tortoises facing each other in a small fountain and connected by a thin stream of water projected from one mouth to the other. Next come the Grotto of Diana and the Grotto of the Goat.

The mechanical theater, near the grottoes, was built by Loriz Rosenegger of Nüremberg. It is much later than the rest of Hellbrunn. It looks like a stone music box, the stage of which is occupied by hundreds of automatons. These

155

Austria

are activated by royal dinner music by Mozart, Lulli, Corelli, and a minor eighteenth-century composer. The inscription engraved on the theater reads: "For the admiration of visitors, for the diversion of youth, for the adornment of the gardens, and as a memento for posterity..." Among the automatons are a grenadier blowing a trumpet and craftsmen doing their work. The sounds accompanying their movements are contrived by water organs, as is the sound of birds in the Grotto of Birds. When the figurines stop moving, a mechanical concert begins along with a water display from a number of jets concealed in the front of the theater and designed to spray those whose attention has been caught by the music and automatons.

Near the theater is the Grotto of the Crown. In the middle of it is a fountain under a vault pierced by a round orifice. A jet of water spouts from the rocks and projects a gold crown or cone-shaped gold object into the air. In the past the crown was replaced on informal occasions by a gold phallus. The jet of water shot up in fits and starts three or four times, raising the object higher and higher until it reached the orifice. Then an explosion would deafen the guests. The erotic water display would then end and the golden piece fall back onto the ground. At that moment the fountain would begin to play and spray the guests.

137. *In the park is a curious nymphaeum called the Grotto of the Crown. A jet of water raises a gold crown toward the orifice in the ceiling where it may be admired by all. In earlier times the cult of Dionysus was associated with the grotto and more honored than the archbishop's claim to nobility. Next to the grotto is a promenade where statues of nymphs and fauns have been placed to praise "the union of heaven and earth, the victory of the arts over animal instincts," according to an official report. Notwithstanding, Hellbrunn is a folly dedicated more to Greek gods than to the Christian God and more to earthly love than divine love. Religious excuses were offered for cultural interest in order to protect the archbishop's reputation.*

Preceding pages:
138. *The Octagonal Hall. Marble and trompe-l'œil frescoes; Italian decor for an Austrian palace.*

139. *The main entrance hall. A castle under the sign of the unicorn.*

140. *Painting of a stag with strange antlers.*   140

141

141. *A heavy cabinet over which hangs a painting of a long fish.*

142. *The marble staircase leading to the state apartments. In the entrance hall is a collection of paintings of fantastic subjects. A horse with eight golden shoes is attended by a Turkish riding master. A tapestry depicts albino animals—deer, stags and rabbits. The castle is a paradise on earth for a hunter of the unusual.*

144. *Archbishop Markus Sittikus in front of a drawing of the plan of Hellbrunn.*

▷ 143. *The main gallery is decorated in an Italian style. The* trompe-l'œil *murals show city streets, Roman trophies, and balconies with figures in perspective.*

Next pages:
145. *An embroidered picture depicting a hunter and his falcon.*

146. *Items connected with hunting. Game-bag, ring, carving knife and fork mounted into the antlers of a deer, sixteenth-century silverware, a horn, and other objects.*

147. *Open-air theater with a table to catch guests unaware. Jets of water spout at will from the benches and table top.*

148. *The Grotto of Neptune features motifs suitable for the mythological god of the sea.*

145

146

147

148

152

152. *The alley of invisible water leading to one of the pavilions in the park. An archway of water was formed for the guests to pass under but the first few were always caught by the rising jets.*

153. *Mannerist and neo-Egyptian entrance to ▷ the Grotto of Neptune.*

153

◁ 151. *On either side of the entrance to the Grotto of Neptune the heads of stags spout water.*

154. *The main fountains in ▷ front of the Grotto of Neptune.*

154

Preceding pages:
149. *Rearing unicorns stand before the main fountain.*

150. *Between obelisks one of the archbishop's greyhounds turns its head toward its master's window.*

155. *The Theater of Automatons, built in the eighteenth century.*

156. *The Grotto and Fountain of the Goat.*

158. *Detail of a fountain and a natural spring with two tortoises, symbols of the earth.*

△
157. *Grotesque figures in an isolated bower.*

159. *Grimacing gnome. This expression has been* ▷ *associated with the world of the Romanesque period.*

160. *Sixteenth-century syncretism. In an Italian fountain the statue of a pagan god for a Catholic Austrian archbishop.*

Next pages:
161. *The Grotto of the Mirrors leads to the Grotto of Birds, seen through the doorway.*

162. *Portrait of Hearst, magnate of the American press. He built the fabled mansion Casa Grande at San Simeon, California.*

163. *Orson Welles in the motion picture Citizen Kane. The role of Kane was based on Hearst.*

164. *From left to right: Hearst, the actress Marion Davies, and Charlie Chaplin. Hearst lavishly entertained the celebrities of Hollywood.*

Hearst and San Simeon

A mansion built in twentieth-century America on the scale of a Renaissance palace.

William Randolph Hearst was a particularly American personality. Perhaps it is peculiarly significant that he inspired the central character in a classic American motion picture, Orson Welles' *Citizen Kane*. Hearst inherited a fortune from his father, who made his money chiefly in mining activities (he was instrumental in discovering the famous Anaconda mine in Montana). In 1887, when he was twenty-four years old, the young Hearst took charge of the San Francisco *Examiner*, owned by his father. This was the first acquisition of the powerful newspaper, magazine, and radio station empire Hearst was later to control. He was fantastically wealthy when he decided to build an elaborate castle called Casa Grande near the little California coast village of San Simeon. It was to be the inspiration of the fictional Xanadu in *Citizen Kane*.

Houses have often been commissioned by dreamers who were born powerful because of wealth and whose preoccupation was the transformation of a fortune into a castle. For Hearst, his castle was to be a place where he could escape from the burden of the world of business. It has been said that the causes he fought for were no less important to him than his passion for Casa Grande, and no one has ever been able to prove that he championed any particular one only out of self-interest. The one certainty is that he defied all challengers because he was always confident that victory would be assured by his newspapers. This confidence was even shared by Hearst's mother who is said to have met the financier Russell Sage one day on Fifth Avenue in New York. At that time Sage reportedly said to Phoebe Hearst: "If your son continues to attack the institutions of Wall Street, he will lose one million dollars a year." She simply replied: "At that rate, he can stay in business another eighty years."

When Hearst decided to build a castle, he had the same fervid determination which marked his crusades in the press. Only now the cause was the satisfaction of his need to create a dream palace.

Casa Grande is undoubtedly one of the strangest follies in the United States. Constructed like a Mudejar palace on a hill, Hearst's castle was lived in between 1925, after three years of construction, and 1951 when Hearst died leaving the castle in what he considered to be an incomplete state, despite its luxurious furnishings.

The architecture, replete with references to various styles, is symbolic of the greedily acquisitive owner who sought art works from many cultures. The façade looks something like the front of a Roman basilica, and is flanked by two bell towers in a Spanish Renaissance style. Each supports eighteen carillon bells cast in Belgium. Covered with white and blue ceramic tiles, the façade also reflects a Moslem inspiration, but the entrance, flanked by statues of Saint Peter and Saint Paul, looks like the portal to a cathedral. Casa Grande was in fact designed by an architect of Berkeley, Julia Morgan, who was a graduate of the Paris School of Beaux-Arts. She was constantly obliged to alter her plans due to numerous changes demanded by Hearst.

Hearst wanted San Simeon to accommodate an endless stream of guests, many of whom were celebrities of the entertainment, sports, and literary worlds, and to provide a setting for a plethora of art objects to which he constantly made new additions. From childhood he had longed to live on the Cuesta Encantada, the Enchanted Hill—the name of the San Simeon property—which his father had bought. His father had acquired 40,000 acres of Pacific coast and a large number of ranches and then increased his holdings by adding San Simeon and Santa Rosa, which were formerly owned by Franciscan missions. From 1870 George Hearst was in the habit of taking his friends and his son, William Randolph, on outings to San Simeon. The party would arrive from Los Angeles by carriage, pitch tents, and camp out for weekends during the good weather. The Enchanted Hill thus became the setting for the elder Hearst's fashionable country gatherings. In 1919 William Randolph Hearst inherited this land and became the owner of the site filled with youthful memories.

Hearst lived in a large New York apartment, but returned periodically to San Simeon. He decided to replace the tent village with a house, or rather a castle, surrounded in a park setting by three guest "cottages" each with ten to eighteen rooms. These cottages, for which he wanted white walls and a Spanish Renaissance ambience, were named according to their location on the San Simeon terrain. La Casa del Monte looked out onto the Santa Lucia mountains; La Casa del Mar provided a panorama of the Pacific; and La Casa del Sol afforded a striking view of the sun as it set over the ocean. These were built from 1919 until 1921, and Hearst occupied La Casa del Mar while Casa Grande was being completed. The Hearst family moved into the great mansion at Christmas time in 1925.

The three cottages and Casa Grande are furnished with an incredible accumulation of art objects, architectural details, furniture, silverware, and china. Carved ceilings and hand-worked mantlepieces, Persian rugs and Roman mosaics give only an indication of the variety of items Hearst imported through the tiny port of San Simeon and had transported up the mountain to the estate. An inventory of the paneled rooms, staircases, and other architectural elements would convey little concept of their actual existence, not to mention the furnishings like tapestries, antique silks, and canopied beds. Hearst visualized San Simeon as a stronghold of pleasure where his guests could find all kinds of amusements. Such were the dreams of a man lost in the tumult of the Roaring Twenties described in the novels of F. Scott Fitzgerald. There was a touch of Gatsby in Hearst who had a great fortune and dreamed of endless parties in a park cultivated on a mountaintop.

Actors and actresses of the motion picture world figured large in the social life of San Simeon, and most of the great names of Hollywood participated at some time in the elaborate entertainments for which no effort and no expense were too great. Life was informal, and the guests amused themselves with an apparently endless stream of diversions. The fancy dress parties, particularly favored by Hearst, indicate a desire for fantasy that is symbolic of the estate. Costumes from motion picture studios in Hollywood as well as makeup artists and hairdressers were provided for the revelers to make the illusion as real as possible.

Other favorite diversions were the picnics which Hearst improvised. These often consisted of horseback outings on which the party could ride for a number of days without leaving the San Simeon property. Preceding the group would be a staff of servants and all the portable equipment and provisions needed for outdoor feasts. Hearst, a strapping six-footer, endowed with a robust physique and an impressive vitality, delighted in leading these expeditions, returning in far better condition than his younger but not so rugged guests.

In the 1930's a private train brought the notables of the motion picture world the two hundred miles from Hollywood to San Simeon. Each Friday evening those invited, the actors and actresses, the stars of the sporting world, the famous and those still unknown, would make the trip. During the journey Hearst provided food, drink, and entertainment. Once the train had reached its destination, a fleet of limousines would be waiting to sweep the guests up to the castle.

Rules and regulations at San Simeon were few. One was that each evening the company gather in what was called the assembly room to be greeted by Hearst. He would descend from his own quarters, the Gothic Suite, in his private elevator to mingle among them. Another was the limit on liquor consumption: one cocktail was allowed before dinner. A guest discovered with liquor in his private rooms was asked to leave.

Apart from the stars of the motion picture world, the guest list over the years included such notables as President and Mrs. Calvin Coolidge, Winston Churchill, Charles Lindbergh, and George Bernard Shaw.

The accommodations at San Simeon included two swimming pools, a dance floor, a zoo, stables, a movie theater, two libraries, and a billiard room. The indoor swimming pool had two tennis courts built atop its roof. Casa Grande, which has no less than one hundred rooms, consisted of a series of suites and comprised thirty-eight bedrooms, fourteen sitting rooms, thirty-one bathrooms, the large drawing room where the guests assembled to be greeted by Hearst, and special facilities like a barber and beauty parlor. The kitchen was planned on a scale suitable for a hotel.

Hearst himself occupied the Gothic Suite, designed in a neogothic style. The bedroom —eighteen by twenty feet—was the smallest in Casa Grande, but the French canopy bed of oak had a different design for each of the hand-carved posts and dated from the fifteenth or sixteenth century. Among the decorations were pictures of Hearst's mother and father and a fourteenth-century painting of the Madonna by the Italian master Segna. In the bathroom the fixtures were gold plated, even the drain pipes.

Hearst chose to have hung on the walls of San Simeon this passage from Edward Bulwer Lytton's *The Lady of Lyons* for it could be a description of his California home:

LA CUESTA ENCANTADA

If thou wouldst have me paint
The home to which could love fulfill its prayers
This hand would lead then listen...
A palace lifting to eternal summer
Its marble walls from out a glossy bower
Of coolest foliage, musical with birds...
And when night came...the perfumed light
Stole through the mists of alabaster lamps
And every air was heavy with the sighs
Of orange groves and music from sweet lutes
And murmurs of low fountains that gush forth
In the midst of moss. Dost thou like the picture?

The outdoor Neptune pool was faced with blue tiles and surrounded by an atrium, a Greek temple, and a dance floor decorated with white marble statues of Neptune and the Nereids. Hearst had it enlarged twice, and its final cost has been estimated at almost $1,000,000. This blue pool, set in an Italian terraced garden, was complemented by the indoor Roman pool. Oscar Lewis, one of Hearst's biographers, wrote that the eclecticism evident at San Simeon in the atmosphere of the main house and evinced here in the decor of the pools recalls the life of the Medici, but in fact, it actually epitomizes a modern concept of luxury. The Roman pool, surrounded by Roman statues, is lined with Venetian glass tiles contrasted with others of 22-carat gold.

Out of the total of some 265,000 acres that finally comprised the property, Hearst had one hundred twenty-three acres cleared on the Enchanted Hill for the grounds of his house. The landscape, which preserved the native oak trees of the site, was studded with azaleas, roses, and jasmine. To keep them alive water was piped from springs five miles away. Many exotic plants were placed in soil compounded to meet their special requirements. Twenty permanent gardeners catered to Hearst's whims regarding the grounds, doing their work at night because Hearst did not like to watch it in progress.

Into this artificial background were placed objects of valuable art, statues, busts, and other works. All were blended into a setting of terraces, balustrades, stairways, and fountains. Mountains rose in the background like a stage set.

Fringed by a strip of coastline between San Francisco and Los Angeles, San Simeon is now frequented by hippies who have discovered, as did Hearst, that no more secluded area, no gentler climate, and no wilder coast exist anywhere.

It was to this glittering setting that the guests arrived, by car, by train, and by airplanes that landed at the private airfield. Although Hearst was often absent, he did all he could to make sure that they would enjoy themselves. He especially liked serving game to his dinner guests. Often numbering in the dozens, they were seated at long tables in the Casa Grande dining room, or Refectory. A staff of sixty servants waited on the guests at tables where they found Victorian silverware, embroidered linen tablecloths, and silver candelabra. Hearst insisted on one convention, the use of paper napkins, which supposedly evoked the rustic life of San Simeon before the construction of Casa Grande. However, one suspects that forces other than sentimentality were at work, for linen napkins were also used, but only when Hearst himself was present.

The customary entertainment after dinner was a motion picture. Hearst arranged to show the most popular films in advance of their release to public theaters.

A listing of the objects at San Simeon would require a ledger. The suites of rooms at Casa Grande were in many instances named after a particular object or piece of furniture, or for some architectural feature. The Duplex Suite had its bed on a balcony with an ornately carved balustrade. The bed was reached by climbing a twisting interior stairway. The carved ceiling has in its center a painting of *The Departure of Venus* by Jean Baptiste Van Loo, a French painter who lived into the eighteenth century.

The Della Robbia Suite had works by the famous family of Italian terra-cotta workers, including a bas-relief of *St. Joseph and the Child* that hung over the French Louis XII fireplace. A painting of the *Immaculate Conception* attributed to the Spanish artist Murillo also hung in this room.

The Doge's Suite, as the name suggests, is Venetian in inspiration. The walls were hung with blue damask, and the ceiling of carved wood and mural paintings was originally in a palace in Venice.

The dining room, or Refectory, looked like a great baronial hall. This effect was achieved by old banners from Siena, by Gothic arch windows, and by the carved sixteenth-century Italian ceiling. Also contributing to the atmosphere were Gothic choir stalls and sixteenth-century Flemish tapestries portraying stories of the life of Daniel. Displayed in this room was Hearst's magnificent collection of antique silver.

The bookcases in the large library contained a collection of rare books that Hearst assembled over a lifetime. On top of the cases stood a collection of ancient Greek vases and other artifacts.

The list runs on seemingly without end: the carved sixteenth-century walnut bed of Cardinal de Richelieu; tapestries by the sixteenth-century Roman artist Giulio Romano and by Peter Paul Rubens; paintings by such diverse artists as the great Spaniard Francisco Goya and the nineteenth-century French Léon Gérome. These and a myriad of others combined with anon-ymous objects like antique Millefleur tapestries and Oriental rugs to create a museum atmosphere that some found overwhelming.

The same eclecticism was evident on the grounds, where statues as diverse as one from the eighteenth dynasty of ancient Egypt shared space with Roman wellheads, reconstructed medieval fountains, and modern copies of works by the great masters of sculpture.

One of the most prodigal creations of the extravagant host of San Simeon was the zoo. This began in 1924 with a herd of pure white fallow deer that he imported from Asia. Eventually some two thousand acres were enclosed, and all types of animals roamed them—buffaloes, kangaroos, antelopes, zebras, ostriches, and llamas, to give a random selection. A place was also provided for caged animals—lions, elephants, and monkeys. At its zenith Hearst's collection rivaled the largest public zoos, and he insisted that all of the inhabitants receive the most careful attention and best diets. Like other men in privileged positions who may have tended to question the motives of those about them, Hearst loved animals. On the tombstone of his dachshund he had inscribed "My dearest friend." In his publications he waged a perennial campaign against vivisection.

Hearst found one disadvantage to his house at San Simeon: it was a distance from Hollywood. To have a more convenient location he had built near Santa Monica a small palace somewhat ingenuously known as the beach house. It contained more than one hundred rooms, and offered guests such choices as swimming in the ocean or pool. When Hearst was there for a weekend, the visitors numbered in the many dozens. Actually the concept of the beach house was quite like that of San Simeon. Both incorporated architectural details from old European buildings, both were furnished with fine works of art, both overflowed with a constantly changing entourage of talented and beautiful visitors who were treated to unending diversions. The attractions ranged from a marble bridge from Venice over the swimming pool to paintings by the old masters. As at San Simeon, Hearst would occasionally tear out a section to have it remodeled to suit his latest whim.

William Randolph Hearst was a phenomenon, as extinct from the world today as the dinosaur. He was a millionaire who spent lavishly on himself and others, amusing himself in what many would call a childlike way. More than one has smiled at this eccentric who played at picnics and costume balls, who wooed motion picture stars, who collected art objects as if they were baubles, and who built a vast estate for his own reasons. But certainly he was not afflicted with the sense of guilt that the rich sometimes bear, and he was not concerned with the cliché that today we call a public image.

It has been estimated that in the 1930's when San Simeon was filled with visitors, the cost per day to run the estate was $5,000. One can only gasp at the thought of the millions lavished on the structures, their furnishings, and their setting. San Simeon shared the extravagance and the artificiality of Louis XIV's Versailles, with their emphasis on diversion and playing at life. Like Louis XIV, Hearst did not live to see the revolution. He died in 1951, still wealthy, still ebullient. Others perhaps lived more wisely and more beneficially for others, but few provided a comparable amount of entertainment.

Today on walking tours of San Simeon, the guides are careful to point out that Hearst had no desire to steal from Europe. More often than not, he had particular objects and furnishings copied rather than taking the originals from their homes. He knew that his taste was indiscriminate, but was not bothered by this. He treated the counterfeit like the genuine, and accepted a lack of talent in some people while courting the gifted.

Mrs. Hearst was convinced that San Simeon was the work of a lunatic. One night after being startled by the howling of an orangutan, she declared: "The whole place is crazy! Look at it! A creation of Otto the Madman... and he will continue to add and refine until the day he dies. What good will it be then? No one can afford to keep it up."

United States

After Hearst's death, the state of California acquired all rights to the castle and opened it to the public in 1958. Zebras and cows, tahr goats and Barbary sheep, these and other exotic animals still graze side by side in the pastures that border the five-mile drive that climbs up from San Simeon. To some a pall hangs over the estate, giving it the atmosphere of a mausoleum. This legendary domain is visited and described in whispers, just as if one were passing through a modern Escorial incorporating aspects of a Mexican cathedral, a Walter Scott castle, and the Villa Medici. Whatever its beauty, hideousness, or symbolic value, every mausoleum exercises a power over the masses, whether it enshrines Lenin, Philip II of Spain, or a titan of the American press. The crowds visiting San Simeon are silent. Some of the visitors, however, do smile at the heterogeneous architecture, the many genuine and false objects, the Greco-Roman temples disassembled and shipped stone by stone, and the vast accumulation of the valuable and insignificant.

As mentioned earlier, Hearst has been compared to Fitzgerald's Gatsby. The two characters, one real, the other fictional, had a common need for building palatial mansions in which to receive the rich and famous of their day although neither could count on being liked by his guests. Today one senses that the crowds that view San Simeon respect the folly of grandeur in an exceptional man, just as the Ancients respected abnormal beings, seeing in them the mark of an extraordinary destiny.

165. *Neo-Greek colonnade around the Neptune pool at Casa Grande.*

167. *Portrait of Hearst at thirty-one by Orrin Peck.*

167

◁ 166. *View of the Neptune pool and its terraced setting.*

168

◁ 168. *The main drawing room.*

172. *A Greco-Roman temple bought in Europe and reas-* ▷
sembled at San Simeon adorns the Neptune pool.

169. *The indoor Roman pool. The ancient world in*
the twentieth century.
▽

169

170

170. *The Neptune pool, with*
mosaic tiling. An Italian villa
transplanted to a mountain land-
scape.

171. *The colonnade seen from*
the dance floor.

171

173. *A guest invited to one of Hearst's parties came through this park and arrived on the scene with his face dripping blood from razor slashes. He claimed to have been attacked while crossing the grounds. After his face had been bandaged, he appeared for dinner and chatted amiably with the other guests. Later the same evening there was a commotion; the man was discovered behind a pillar, his bandages ripped and his face bloody from fresh razor slashes. He claimed to have been attacked again, but he had in fact been slashing himself. The man had been trying to attract attention in a place where people were dominated by the decor.*

174. *Renaissance bed at Casa Grande.* ▷

175. *A park for a man who owned one of America's great fortunes. Shortly after Hearst's death San Simeon was acquired by the State of California and opened to the public. No one could afford to maintain it after Hearst died.*
▽

174

175

The Shell Cottage and
the Dairy at Rambouillet

Two settings in which noblewomen played at being shepherdesses. Here Marie Antoinette and the Princess de Lamballe amused themselves until the French Revolution.

Marie Antoinette, Queen of France, and her companion the Princess de Lamballe were destined to die tragically. In life they sought to amuse themselves at the château of Rambouillet, some thirty miles southwest of Paris. The château is architecturally uninteresting, although filled with historical and literary associations. Its park is of notable loveliness.

A previous owner of this turreted house was the Duc de Montausier, model for Alceste in Moliere's *Le Misanthrope*. The Duc de Montausier had the garden designed in the French classical style which Louis XIV liked, but which had become out of date under Louis XV.

The young and widowed Princess de Lamballe lived there with her father-in-law, Louis Jean Marie de Bourbon, Duc de Penthièvre. The presence of the young widow helped him to forget his own sorrow: the loss of his son and of his wife, Marie Thérèse d'Este, Princess of Modena.

These sad memories had for a time kept the duke from the château which he had inherited from his parents, the Comte de Toulouse, son of Louis XIV and Mme de Montespan. His father was Grand Admiral of France. Thanks to the influence of his mother, the comtesse, with

Louis XV, his father had been able to expand and reconstruct Rambouillet. The Comte de Toulouse, knowing that his son would inherit the title of Grand Admiral, had dug a canal on which he launched a flotilla worthy of a future admiral.

After the death of her dissolute husband, the Princess de Lamballe, in accordance with the etiquette of the time, withdrew to mourn, retiring to the convent of Les Dames de la Rue Saint-Antoine. While waiting for the princess, who was to become the life and soul of the bleak château, to return, her father-in-law, now the Grand Admiral, spent his time on his large estate. She finally rejoined the old, austere, and distinguished gentleman, who was as virtuous as his son had been decadent.

The princess was pathologically sensitive. She was known to faint at the smell of a bouquet of violets. Often she was lifeless and lethargic. The remedies that she needed were not to be discovered for another century in new studies of psychological disorders. Her anxious father-in-law did his utmost to amuse her. For her sake he yielded to the anglophilia of the time and planted near the classical French garden an informal "true garden of nature," or

191

176. *This thatched cottage in the park at Rambouillet was built for the Princess de Lamballe. Inside is a room whose walls are covered with sea shells.*

France

English garden. The current vogue reflected the influence of Jean Jacques Rousseau, who urged a return to simple life. In the garden were built what were then called *fabriques*, or false pavilions, a counterfeit thatched cottage and a fake hermitage.

Since a passion for the pastoral and rustic had become a trait of the times, it was fashionable to eulogize simple village life and despise grandeur in the midst of luxury. The return to nature advocated by Rousseau, the reading of English and German writers and the Swiss poet Gessner, and an expressed admiration for manual labor, all contributed to a relaxation of etiquette, which was to be encouraged by Marie Antoinette.

In marked contrast to its thatched roof, the cottage had a handsome salon whose walls were faced with sea shells. The little building was an enchanted retreat, where love of what was imagined to be the pastoral life was blended with the desire for a fairy-tale existence. The occupants played Cinderella not in a dingy kitchen but in an elegant drawing room made of shellwork. The effect of this salon in the thatched-roof cottage is still surprising, and one tends to forget the brutal end of the girl who was the first to see and enjoy it.

The marriage of the Dauphin of France, the future Louis XVI, to Marie Antoinette, Archduchess of Austria, was celebrated at Versailles on May 16, 1770. The new queen spoke little French, but knew Italian, which she had learned from the Roman poet Metastasio. Marie Antoinette soon noticed a girl not unlike herself —a twenty-year-old princess with flaxen hair and milk-white skin, who also spoke Italian, for the Princess de Lamballe had been born in Turin.

After being chosen as a suitable companion for Marie Antoinette, the princess sped by carriage from Rambouillet escorted by her father-in-law's servants. The queen liked her, despite her peculiarities, headaches, and fainting spells caused by the sight of a spider, a crayfish, or a lobster.

The queen appointed the princess stewardess of the royal household. This was no mere sinecure, for she had to submit the queen's requests for money to unsympathetic ministers, and try to persuade such recalcitrant financial administrators as Jacques Necker and Anne Robert Turgot in favor of the queen's desires to renovate, embellish, and transform Versailles according to the current fashion. Although Mme de Lamballe, who had learned grand manners from her father-in-law the Duc de Penthièvre, proved a skillful ambassadress, the queen was fickle. A rival, Mme de Polignac, soon undermined Mme de Lamballe's prestige. The princess returned to Rambouillet, where her father-in-law vainly tried once again to amuse her. Her nervous disorders grew worse. She sought remedies, going to spas like Plom-

The Shell Cottage and the Dairy at Rambouillet

bières and Bourbonne. She consulted the notorious Franz Mesmer, and was "magnetized" in front of his tub of iron filings and powdered glass.

Then her luck returned; the queen in search of a loyal friend recalled Mme de Lamballe. She was thirty-six. Less timid but still fragile, she fell prey to the influence of the queen, who "magnetized" her more effectively than Mesmer's tub. To help Marie Antoinette forget the formal life of Versailles, she offered the queen the opportunity to amuse herself at Rambouillet. Yielding to the insistence of Marie Antoinette, Louis XVI bought the estate in 1783 from the Duc de Penthièvre for 18,000,000 francs. The queen thought that the forest of Rambouillet would, moreover, please the king, who was a great huntsman, like all the Bourbons. Louis XVI was also interested in agriculture and shortly after buying Rambouillet installed a model farm, with a flock of Merino sheep from Segovia, to initiate a plan so that France would no longer be dependent on Spain for a supply of high-quality wool.

The king, ever anxious to please his wife, commissioned the architect Thévenin to build an elegant little building baptized the "dairy" for his "shepherdess-queen." Louis XVI had a vast store of indulgence and generosity for the whims of Marie Antoinette, which her mother, Maria Theresa, had never encouraged and which were still less sanctioned by her brother, the Emperor Joseph, who deplored the undecorous behavior of the young queen of France. In his opinion she had broken all the traditions of royal Austria. But Marie Antoinette was determined to change the tedium of court life. She would have preferred not dressing in front of several ladies-in-waiting and dispensing with morning courtesy visits, presentations, curtsies, Tuesday ambassadorial receptions, Thursday receptions for old people of the court, and ceremonial Sunday dinners. She would have also preferred to forego public meals with the king and tedious suppers every night with Monsieur, the king's brother.

Marie Antoinette's "dairy" was a small temple of antique inspiration hidden by the shrubbery of the English garden. This temple was decorated with grisaille symbols of the four seasons painted by Pierre Sauvage. A room faced with white marble opened onto a grotto with a statue of a nymph riding a she-goat.

Even the king fell in with the game of playing the simple life. In Michel Sedaine's "Le Roi et le Fermier," in which the queen played the role of a shepherdess, the king sang the following air:

> *What a joy, what a pleasure to read*
> *In the eyes of his fond subjects*
> *Everything inspired by*
> *The presence of a beloved king.*

France

The two noblewomen sought in the cottage and the dairy the pleasure of escape, that break with the ordinary which is the essence of diversion. Some privileged people spent fantastic sums to enjoy the illusion of possessing something lacking in their lives—simplicity. Perhaps only the queen sincerely experienced this need, which sometimes induced her to invite a peasant girl to dine with her daughter; she expected the small royal princess to serve her guest first. Colas, Rose, Colin, and Colette, pastoral roles in plays by Michel Sedaine, Louis Anseaume, and Jean Jacques Rousseau played by the queen, her ladies, and young noblemen of the court, were not, however, the "fond subjects" of the king's air. They were soon cruelly to recall to their masters that life is not a capricious game for everyone.

Fate was soon to catch up with the two princesses of the shell cottage and the dairy at Rambouillet. In 1789 a Revolutionary mob escorted the royal family from Versailles to Paris. There, on August 10, 1792, the Princess de Lamballe was in the queen's apartment when a crowd invaded the Tuileries Palace. She and the queen were taken along with the king, others of the royal family, and a few loyal attendants, to the Legislative Assembly in the garden of the Tuileries. The body was in session in the Manège, the former riding school of the palace. The Princess de Lamballe had a nervous attack, screamed, and fainted.

For three days the noble group lived crammed together in three small rooms, then a coach drove them to the prison of the Temple. Sitting in front, the Princess de Lamballe was exposed to the insults of the crowd. Three days later, she was separated from the queen, who embraced her for the last time. A carriage took her to the Petite Force Prison in the Marais. Another way of the cross; another nervous attack. At dawn on September 3, 1792, suffering from her afflictions, she was unable to go with the men sent by her father-in-law to rescue her. Shortly after she was dragged to the Grande Force Prison and led before an alleged court of law, which gave her over to the mob in the narrow Rue du Roi-de-Sicile. Her head was hacked off with an ax against the corner-post of the Rue des Ballets; then crowned with roses and powdered, it was displayed on the end of a pike in front of the Temple; recognizing it, the queen fainted.

The Princess de Lamballe's thatched cottage and Marie Antoinette's dairy are today the relics of two overly impressionable women and of the world they lived in. They remind us that this world had lovely things.

177. *Princess de Lamballe, who loved follies,* ▷
and revered Marie Antoinette.

178. *The head of Princess de Lamballe on a* ▷
pike, her body mutilated and torn on the ground.

177

178

179. *The central motif of a medallion in the*
salon of the shellwork inside the thatched cottage
at Rambouillet. Arturo Lopez, one of the patrons
restoring Versailles, obtained the right to repro-
duce this salon in his Paris mansion, according
to reports, by agreeing to defray the cost of
restoring the cottage. After the death of Lopez,
his mansion was demolished and the salon
destroyed.
▽

180. *A cup belonging to Marie An-*
toinette.

180

181. *A porcelain mug used to drink*
fresh milk at Rambouillet.

181

Next pages:
182. *The salon of shellwork. The*
rocaille furniture designed for the cur-
ved sections of the room still exists.

179

◁ 183. *The so-called dairy in the form of an ancient temple was designed for Marie Antoinette by the architect Thévenin, who was influenced by Claude Ledoux.*

184. *Inside the dairy a white marble room with a marble table leads to a grotto with the statue of a nymph. When Marie Antoinette played here, she served her guests milk from containers that were part of the decor.*

The "Desert" of Retz

Near Paris in a decaying domain stand the remains of a strange house in the form of a truncated column.

A few more years and the "Desert" will be no more than a poem in the likeness of an era. But how splendid to preserve from an era a poem!

—Colette

On the confines of the forest of Marly, not far from Saint-Germain-en-Laye, in the parish of Chambourcy, in France, a great crumbling wall embraces a decaying domain consisting of a Temple of Rest, a Chinese pavilion, a Temple of Pan, and a dwelling in the form of a truncated column. Today these are all covered with vines and other plants. This is the "Desert" of Retz, which apparently got its name from the owner's desire to be isolated. The site is only some twenty miles from Paris, however, and is not difficult to travel to today.

Not too long ago Hans Arp, the surrealist artist, entered the Desert as if into a dream and recognized:

The white hair of stone, the black hair of water,
The green hair of children, the white hair of eyes.

With this in mind one may go there in search of the eccentric who, before the surrealists and the symbolists, even before the roman-tics and their taste for ruins, sought out the lugubrious possibilities of civilizations past and future.

Is the Desert of Retz an inspired poem or a vapid elegy? It is a bit of both. The name of its creator, François Nicolas Racine du Jonquoi, Seigneur du Thuit, Baron de Monville, is little known. He was born in Alençon in 1730, became Grand-Master of Waters and Forests in 1757, acquired the property of Retz (the park covers some sixty-five acres) in 1774, and proceeded to enlarge and embellish it for a decade.

The vogue of his period was for theaters in gardens, mazes, and temples dedicated to love or friendship, but not yet for ruins. In the middle of the century of enlightenment, however, Monville decided to build a second life out of his dreams. Until then imagination had not appeared an important quality to eighteenth-century society, which rewarded talent practicing the principles of freethinking. Claude Crébillon fils became famous for such works as *Le Sopha*, which were light and agreeable in tone, but had nothing suggestive about them except the title. Denis Diderot bowed to the prevailing mode in *Les Bijoux Indiscrets*. Many other lesser writers were read because they

185. *The Desert of Retz: the Temple of Love on the edge of the Forest of Marly miraculously escaped destruction during the Revolution.*

appealed to the senses rather than the heart, "a faculty which we are progressively losing out of disuse," wrote René Louis d'Argenson in his *Mémoires*. In every age, some people are unaffected by fashion and, among them, was the young Monville, who wanted to give more substance to his secret longings than those of people skimming the surface of life without touching it like skaters in a contemporary print with the caption: "Glide on, oh mortals, do not linger."

Jean Jacques Rousseau had combined philosophical reflection with a gift for feeling in *La Nouvelle Héloïse*. The style of life was changing in the third quarter of the eighteenth century; ladies were beginning to like country life; botany was becoming a popular pastime with the gentry; men and women of fashion were discovering the joys of rustic retreats on the banks of the Seine and the Marne; and Diderot was exploring the outskirts of Paris. Country luncheon parties were arranged; landscape designers and gardeners were called from England to create parks in which, in Diderot's phrase, "nature was everywhere apparent." Monville, a man of the world, no doubt also sensed the urge to return to nature, but he wanted to make nature the accomplice not of his love affairs, as she was to many, but of a metaphysical dream. Fashionable life could only frustrate this concept, which in a sense is symbolized by the broken columns dear to his visions.

The impression made by this rich and seductive young man can easily be recaptured. An anecdote told by the author Nicolas Sébastien de Chamfort reveals his reputation at Versailles and, above all, his well-turned legs. "One day King Louis XV said to Mme d'Esparbès: 'You have slept with all my subjects.' 'Oh! Sire!' 'You have had the Duc de Choiseul.' 'He is so strong.' 'The Maréchal de Richelieu.' 'He is so witty.' 'Monville.' 'He has such handsome legs!'" However, Monville did have other assets. He played the harp well enough to accompany Gluck and Monsigny. He delighted and changed his mistresses often, snatching a young lady of the Opera from a Farmer-General. M. de Sartine, the head of the Paris police, necessarily kept an eye on him. He was an excellent archer, surprising the Prince of Nassau on one occasion and, on another, the Duc de Chartres, the future Duc d'Orléans, who became his friend and guest at the Desert of Retz. The duke had challenged him to shoot a pheasant in flight with ten arrows. "At the first shot, the bowman hit the bird, but missed with the other nine," wrote an observer.

Monville, then in his forties, had lived from the age of twenty in Paris on the Rue Neuve-des-Petits-Champs, where his father, the rich Jean Baptiste Racine du Jonquoi, General Tax Collector and, subsequently, General Treasurer of Public Works, had sent him to live with his grandfather Le Monnier. His past as a young dandy, serenading such ladies as Mme Brissard or the actress Astraudy beneath their windows until chased away by the watch, still clung to this man of whom his friend Dufort de Cheverny wrote: "He amazed in every accomplishment, riding, playing tennis and musical instruments, or in archery which he knew better than a savage... Brother of the Marquise of Revel, this young man, who was a few years older than I, was one of the most handsome gentlemen in Paris. He was five feet six inches tall. Built like a model, he had a fine figure, superb legs, and a slightly small but agreeable head. He was a superior dancer and was forever receiving invitations to all the balls." This portrait, however, was not enough to make this young man an ambassador and Dufort de Cheverny was appointed over Monville, "whose father was not well connected and whose grandfather had no title but a large fortune."

We do know that by marrying Mlle Aimable Charlotte Lucas de Boncourt in 1755, M. de Monville was able to embellish the wedding announcement with titles he had not had until that year. Had he acquired them in the meantime? Monville became a Seigneur du Thuit, Baron de Monville and was married for only a short time. Charlotte died two years later in 1757 and he became Grand-Master of Waters and Forests in Rouen. Monville

lived part of the time at Le Thuit, part of the time in Paris. Married but soon a widower, unfavored at court, Monville frequented the fashionable Faubourg-Saint-Germain. Here he often spent time at the home of Mme de Genlis on the Rue de Bellechasse, playing the harp, dining, and conversing. But Monville had to cross the Seine to return to his townhouse on the Rue d'Anjou. There, in the solitude of the great mansion designed by Étienne Louis Boullée, precursor of Claude Nicolas Ledoux and, like him, an architectural visionary, the Grand-Master of Waters and Forests withdrew to muse. His library contained many works, on the cultivation of trees, horticulture, and botany. These books were later to be taken to Retz. There, he would discuss his schemes with Boullée and they would contemplate a decorative setting different from the sumptuous residence of the Rue d'Anjou. This was demolished during the construction of the Boulevard Malesherbes and only one engraving of the house (in the French National Library's Print Department) survives.

The description written by Dufort de Cheverny, who tried to persuade Monville to buy his post of ambassador, provides an idea of the urbane and theatrical splendor in which the future builder of picturesque decay lived:

"I climbed eight steps and entered a very hot stucco waiting room furnished with a magnificent stove. A valet opened and closed the double doors, and I found myself in a gilded antechamber lit by a chandelier with eight candles and by six pairs of candelabra with three branches. At the far end I saw an impressive sideboard laden with finery; a clock chimed and, through the paneling, came the concerted strains of a piece by Rameau for several instruments. I passed into a first salon adorned with projecting columns, brilliant with concealed lights and resplendent as a sunlit day. I continued and came to a most elegant bedroom, all in crimson velvet fringed with gold. I had never before seen anything so splendid. Everything was illuminated, everything revealed, and I was alone. I imagined myself in a fairyland palace or in a palace from the Arabian Nights. I proceeded into another room and saw Monville, superbly dressed, posed writing in front of a porcelain desk, exquisitely handsome and pleasing. The study was open on two sides and the heating flues were so well placed that, although it was cold outside, it felt like midsummer. Not a fireplace in sight; everything was heated by stoves fed and tended out of view. The next room was a windowless Turkish salon lined with mirrors and lit by a skylight. A projecting balustrade in the finest taste arched over the salon, which had a thick Turkish carpet. In the center was a crimson velvet ottoman fringed with gold, with no woodwork, on which large Italian taffeta cushions were scattered at will to make a

higher seat or supports for the back or the arms. In the background was another ottoman, richer still if that were possible. The doors of this enchanting retreat moved in slots conforming to the shape of the room. A secret device in the wall, when lightly pressed, opened them with marvelous expedition. Soon I was to hear above my head a concert of wind instruments—a fashion from Germany, then in vogue with princes and ambassadors at supper parties." This description reflects the luxurious atmosphere, with its Oriental outlandishness, mechanical ingenuities, tricks of illusion, and vanishing doors, which seem to have been particularly popular with many international aesthetes in the eighteenth century.

In 1774, at the age of forty-four, Monville acquired from a M. Bazise the right of use of a country house at Retz. From then until 1786 he enlarged the property and formed a park that was haunted by his ivy-entwined apocalyptic structures: a dwelling in the form of ruins, the Temple of Rest, and other allusions to death. These works are surprising perhaps in a rake known for his sensual tastes; nothing had suggested a man fascinated by the transcendent. In Monville, however, a predilection for alcoves seems to have been combined with one for cemeteries.

Monville's friend Boullée helped him in the realization of Retz, undoubtedly designing some of the structures, including the truncated column. We know that a certain Barbier, a former student at the Academy, prepared the plans for the Chinese pavilion and supervised its execution. A lawsuit in 1780 dealing with the fees claimed by Barbier provides some relevant information. According to the record of the proceedings, Barbier did little work on the other pavilions. Monville himself designed most of the structures, for which he had clay models made. It was with Barbier's help, however, that the Chinese pavilion, now completely fallen into ruins, the icehouse, some architectural trellis-work, the painted iron obelisk, and the tent were built.

An inventory and engravings provide an idea of the former state of this domain. The obelisk, the hermitage, and the tomb on the southern part of the estate no longer exist. The former dairy and the share-holding farms are in ruins; the cottage, orangery, and greenhouses of Lerouge's prints have disappeared.

In the northern part a wooden diamond-pointed doorway marked the boundary with the adjoining royal forest. The park was planted with rare trees, and grottoes were formed out of rocks. In 1777 Monville appropriated the thirteenth-century church of Retz, already swathed in ivy to his liking. Of the Temple of Rest only a door and some columns survive. The Temple of Pan, with its colonnade backed against an arched stretch of walls, is standing.

The icehouse was used to store ice for drinks and food, though it was ultimately intended to serve as a tomb. It was once a pyramid surrounded by poplars, but today is nothing more than an ivy-covered heap of stones near the Temple of Pan. The theater stage is identifiable only by some Chinese vases half hidden in the brambles.

The three-tiered Chinese pavilion, on the edge of a pond, had a "charming bit of garden," according to the Prince de Ligne, "which an Emperor of China would have acknowledged." The teakwood structure survived until 1962, when it collapsed. On the ground one can still see parts of the carved walls, recalling the Ming follies of China. Chinese figures decorated the outside of the building. On the roof one of them stood leaning over the balustrade, another held a lantern, and a third a parasol with little bells. Smoke escaped through chimneys topped by painted iron vases serving as flues. Lerouge's floor plans show divans on each floor recessed into alcoves; there was one in the salon which was covered with white flowered paper, and one in the library. The latter was linked to the salon by a secret staircase. Visitors who used it when coming to take tea in Chinese cups in a room filled with jade were fascinated by a mechanical toad.

Laborde thought little of the pavilion although "it once had a great reputation" nor did he like the truncated column. The Prince de Ligne compared it to the Tower of Babel

—the sort of work which "provoked the wrath of God." "The column, broken at the top and 48 feet in diameter, in which Monville has devised a perfect distribution of rooms, is completely his own idea.... It is higher on one side and, from this side, one sees an immense sub-foundation which gives the impression of a height great enough to incur God's jealousy as did the tower of his first children."

This cylindrical foundation is enormous in proportion to the fluted column. The structure is pierced by oval and rectangular windows, through which creepers have penetrated to a central spiral staircase opening onto small rooms disposed according to a circular plan. Trees still conceal the dwelling. The top of the column was designed as a ruin covered with plants as it is today. An underground passage connected the column with an eighteenth-century thatched cottage, painted Pompeian red, which housed service rooms. The column itself had three stories of suites. On the ground-floor, the salon, the dining room, the main bedroom, and the balustrade of the entrance, lined with earthenware vases of plants—heliotropes, geraniums, carnations, periwinkles, and arum lilies. On the other floors were a laboratory, a servant's bedroom, and a studio with a conical skylight, recessed and below the level of the coping of the ruinous walls. All the furniture was carved in wood mostly painted gray and covered with toile de Jouy; the curtains were made of a plain fabric bordered with the same toile de Jouy in Indian patterns; the backs of the alcoves were hung with cloth or wallpaper; mirrors were placed to reflect the garden; the sconces were of gilded bronze and the fireplaces of white marble; and a few mahogany pieces complemented the gray-lacquered furniture. The engravings and pictures listed in the inventory included a Van Loo seascape, a Hubert Robert *Pont de Neuilly*, and family portraits as well as Sèvres porcelain and bronze pieces on the furniture.

Exotic and common trees were planted in the park. Colette refers to this in *Les Paradis terrestres:* "From the threshold the plants appropriating the solidity of stone are more pervasive than seasonal luxuriance permits elsewhere. The grass has everywhere grown a yard high except where trees have stemmed its tide. Beneath an unmoving storm, blue and louring, they ripen and ferment, emitting an awesome scent, fresh humus, half-dead petals, clover, mint, privet, a hint of the perfume which lingers after burials too lavishly flower-strewn... A pond is but a field of rush spears, iris blades, a damp, infested snare..."

M. de Monville summered in the truncated column of the Desert of Retz, and here received Jacques de Tilly, Claude Dorat ("the writer who was always producing and never correcting"), and the Duc d'Orléans. Marie Antoinette, it is said, came to find ideas for the

Trianon. Monville was now about fifty and, according to Tilly, "combined the greatest elegance of manners with the finest breeding. He had a sound, if not profound, intelligence. He was one of those mediocre men, who, nonetheless, have what it takes to spend their lives with the most distinguished people of their day and be liked by them. He had an honest heart and was not corrupted by the ostentation and splendor about him."

While at the Desert of Retz, M. de Monville painted and designed his follies and studied models of them. An easel has been found as has a mobile forge. The small salons hung with toile de Jouy were the setting for gallant and charming occasions. He applied himself to botany and ordered rare trees. At the public auction which followed the sequestration of his property, the choicest specimens from his greenhouses were reserved for the Paris Botanical Gardens.

In 1790 Monville was forced by the Revolution to renounce the way of life which nourished his architectural creation. His sole concern now was to save his skin by emigrating; and he tried to sell both the town house on the Rue d'Anjou and the Desert of Retz. Among the potential buyers of the town house was the playwright Pierre Caron de Beaumarchais, but the price of 400,000 pounds seemed too high to him. In 1792 an Englishman, Lewis Disney Ffytch, bought the Desert for 108,000 pounds,

but it was quickly sequestered as the property of a British *émigré*. After passing through various hands, it was repurchased by Ffytch in 1816 and sold by his heirs in 1827. A hundred years later, the property was a guest house. In 1939 the Desert was classified as a historical monument.

Monville would have settled for less. For him it was enough to have saved his skin by hiding on the Rue de Clichy, where he welcomed revolutionaries and the Duc d'Orléans, the cousin of Louis XVI, who was elected as deputy of Paris to the Convention. This member of the royal family voted the death of the king and was, in turn, guillotined in November, 1793, "when his company had become a reproach," as Tilly wrote. Talleyrand mentions Monville in 1793 among the transient acquaintances of the duke and the Abbé de Montgaillard records that Monville was with the duke when the latter learned that the Convention had decreed his arrest.

"Good God," exclaimed the duke, striking his forehead, "is it possible! After the proofs of patriotism that I have given, after all the sacrifices that I have made, to treat me in this way. What ingratitude! How appalling! What do you say, Monville?"

Monville, according to Montgaillard, was squeezing a lemon over a sole he was preparing to eat. "It is terrible, my Lord," was his reply, "but what can you expect? They have

France

no further use for Your Highness, and are simply doing with you what I am doing with this lemon squeezed of all its juice." So saying, he threw the two halves of the lemon into the fire, remarking to the prince that "sole must be eaten hot..."

Monville succeeded in hiding himself better and avoiding worry. He died in his bed in April, 1797, after, wrote Tilly, "sacrificing himself to all the girls, a different one every night."

Such was the destiny of the creator of the Desert of Retz, the man who had "what it takes to spend his life with... distinguished

people... and be liked by them," as Tilly had written. What had inspired his determination to build ruins with elements devised by the Ancients? To confront the chaos of the world with a measure of order? To suggest a calculated irony would imply a profundity that Monville did not actually possess. Of his dreams there remain only the Temple of Pan and the truncated column; vestiges of the Chinese pavilion lie in or about the pond. The trees and creeping vines have closed over the remains of these follies as though over a forbidden kingdom lost in a jungle.

186. *The dwelling fashioned in the form of a truncated column is one of the rare examples of fantastic architecture in France.*

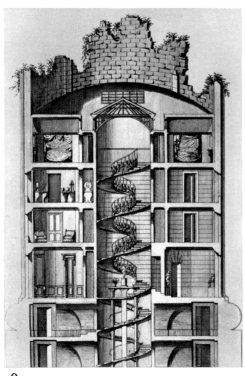

187

◁ 187. *Cross section of the truncated column.*

189. *An engraving depicting the column as it looked when inhabited during the Romantic period. Later the floor collapsed. An artificial ruin became an actual ruin.* ▷

188. *The column, which rested on a Doric base, imitated a real fluted column.* ▽

188

Colonne. Planche VIIe

Élévation Géométrale.

190. *The stairway inside the truncated column.*

191. *Detail of the Chinese pavilion.*

192. *Cross-section of the Chinese*
pavilion showing a bedroom, a salon,
and a library.

193. *The Temple of Pan.*

◁ 194. *The icehouse, originally designed as a tomb, was used to conserve ice for drinks and sherbet served during the summer. The ice was brought from the Alps in the winter and stored in this pyramid. Ice was conserved in the same way at Versailles.*

195. *The icehouse today.*

The Bird's Dream

An anti-palace conceived by the sculptor Niki de Saint-Phalle for a German playwright and stage director, Rainer von Diez.

The Bird's Dream was born of the meeting of Rainer von Diez, the German playwright and stage director, and Niki de Saint-Phalle, the French sculptor noted for her figures of gigantic females that she calls Nanas.

During the early stages of his Munich production of *Lysistrata*, Rainer von Diez saw a photo of her immense sculpture known as the Nana-cathedral, then in Stockholm, and immediately decided to replace the traditional Greek temple of Aristophanes' play with a giant female Nana stretched out on the stage. This woman would be an ideal "temple" allowing the actors to speak from inside the body or the various levels of the outer surface. Niki de Saint-Phalle eventually created a Nana-temple for Rainer von Diez's production, and was subsequently to construct a group of houses in the likeness of a dream for the German director.

The first sections of this residence now stand in the hills of Provence in France. Each room is a separate house covered with polyester vegetation and alive with sculptured representations of strange creatures and human forms. When referring to these unusual houses Niki de Saint-Phalle evokes an incomplete and continuing dream for, as she says, "there will always be new elements to add to this ever-changing

series of sculptured houses that develop as though they were a living being."

The meeting of Rainer von Diez and Niki de Saint-Phalle was thus the inspiration for the creation of the reclining woman, pierced by doors and windows, used as the set of *Lysistrata* and for the unusual residence in the hills of southern France called the *Rêve de l'Oiseau*, the Bird's Dream.

Remembering the inception of this dream the sculptor Jean Tinguely relates: "Niki told Rainer about her future plans. She eventually began to describe a home she wanted to construct and Rainer said to her, 'Build it for me.' Niki declared, 'It will be a spider.' Rainer was not scared and Niki ultimately did as she wanted."

"I have made a spider," she explains, "which will be Rainer's bedroom. The spider is still unpainted and I do not know what color it will be." "It must be black," declared Tinguely; "Niki will paint it green or pink, but will finally admit that a spider must be black. She always ends up painting certain things black."

Continuing her dream, Niki says, "On the roof there will be a spider whose legs ensnare a bride wearing a dress decorated with objects

217

196. *Niki de Saint-Phalle holding the hand of one of her giant Nanas.*

similar to those I have previously sculptured."

At present the only evidence of a spider in the pine grove is two round mounds corresponding to the head and body. To one side and several yards away stand a square house and a blockhouse which have yet to be painted.

"The spider," continues Niki, "will house the bedroom. The other house will be the kitchen. Rainer has always maintained that he wants the interiors to be as empty as a low-rent apartment but they will probably be filled with unusual objects animated by elements of everyday life."

A few months later the spider project was transformed when Niki de Saint-Phalle decided to use only the head and belly of the spider structures as a bathroom, bedroom, and two-faced sphinx. The bathtub will be a concave Nana sunk in the bathroom floor.

Niki de Saint-Phalle has always thought of the Bird's Dream as a paradise built to Rainer's specifications, but, as she says, "It may become something else."

Rainer's home is in a state of evolution and Niki dreams of what might have been as though past possibilities may still be realized. "We could have made a completely narcissistic bedroom for Rainer," she says, "molded to the shape of his face for example. We could have made reproductions of his writings or a plaster bed and chairs with imaginary human figures; we could have installed strange animal figures

in the bathtub or in the bedroom. We might also have fabricated a giant range for the kitchen equipped with oversized everyday household objects." Niki likes Claes Oldenburg's sculptures and says of them: "I am sensitive to them because they have a direct relationship with our childhood world. Objects used by adults always seem oversized to the eyes of a child. In creating his objects Oldenburg has merely remembered objects as he perceived them during his childhood. When I was a child I saw a great many crucifixes and religious icons; I made use of these early perceptions in my later creations. This seems to be the role of childhood in creative adult life as expressed in paintings and sculptures."

For Niki de Saint-Phalle nothing is unchanging and memory or imagination continually nourish her dreams. The world of childhood is always sensibly present to an adult and for an artist memories of disproportions assigned by the perception and imagination of a child often surge into his creations, thus generating a new reality: the realm of dreams or of memories of objects deformed by fear or by their particular emotional importance. The plastic sandwiches, noses, hands, and giant lipsticks created by Oldenburg are merely the same objects as seen by a child. The world Alice encountered in Wonderland is ultimately no more than just such a secondary reality.

Niki continues her description of her dream

composed of sculptured houses: "I would like people to be able to stroll around these houses constantly discovering new aspects and never perceiving the whole at one time." Some time ago when speaking of the kitchen-house covered by strange polyester forms and crowned by a gigantic bird, whence the name Bird's Dream, Niki said: "I installed an artificial woman on one side of this house. Next to her a chair is set against the wall facing the bedroom-house. One side of the kitchen-house will look out onto the hills. Rainer appreciates views while I prefer looking out onto a bare wall, which may be painted or covered with relief sculpture and may not be seen from the outside. The view Rainer has chosen is fine.

"On the wall facing the vista there is a large serpent surrounded by various objects. On one side a man and woman lie in bed still barely outlined since this scene, like the others, is still unpainted. Once painted, the blankets, sheets, and heads will be clearly visible. To the other side of the serpent stands a table covered in polyester and laid with authentic tableware: a fork, a knife, an ashtray, a glass, and a celluloid doll. The third wall is still incomplete."

Niki de Saint-Phalle has transformed the initial plans for the kitchen-house. "At one time we wanted it to be white," says Rainer, "but we finally decided to make it more ominous, more mysterious, and more sinister. The façade will be covered with many objects such as animals, spiders, glasses, and pistols; it will be baroque in style and completely gilded. The kitchen-house will then resemble a threatening yet magical Indian temple."

"Yes," says Niki, "the kitchen-house, once destined to be white, will be golden since we decided that white would connote something too pure and evoke a beautiful but tiring image. The golden surface will be strewn with objects in all imaginable colors. I am going to monstrosify this façade to create a more terrifying, less accessible, and more mysterious appearance. I will add flowers and, were it not for fear of vandalism, I would apply crosses and perhaps a crucifix. Since I am still unsatisfied, I am tantalized by the idea of using objects as perceived during my childhood, among them many religious items. I had wanted to make a huge gilded man but I eventually rejected this idea.

"On the third wall of the kitchen-house," continues Niki, "there will be a sculptured reproduction of a bourgeois bedroom with pieces of furniture set into the wall and wallpaper that I will paint myself, probably in stripes, decorated with celluloid flowers. Human figures in polyester will sit in chairs set against the wall. We might even install real chairs to be used by Rainer and his friends.

"The ensemble will be like the stage setting of a domestic interior based on collected furnishings: a dining room table, wicker armchairs, and assorted picture frames. The

France

sphinx bedroom-house will be visible from the other side.

"The history of this home is difficult to recount because this 'dream' is organic and thus constantly changing. A path leads past the sphinx to an immense head, draped with polyester hair, which houses the toilet. The entrance is set in the midst of flowing tresses. I would also like to scatter trees and animals made of polyester or cement in the surrounding pine woods. I could make any number of objects out of these materials. Perhaps this project will never be completed. This is a home built for a friend, one thing among others, inspired by the Nana-cathedral I created for the Stockholm exhibition and which generated Rainer's new conception of his production of *Lysistrata*. He is not only a stage director, but also a playwright. We are co-authors of *Ich (Me)* which was produced in Kassel, Germany."

Niki de Saint-Phalle passes from one Nana to the next, from the memory of a gigantic woman to plans for future projects. "The Bird's Dream was ultimately," says Niki, "contained in the Stockholm Nana-cathedral. I baptized this particular Nana, created with the help of Tinguely and Ultvedt, *Nana Hon* (hon means "she" in Swedish), but eventually she came to be known as the Nana-cathedral since she represented an actual modern cathedral.

"The Nana-cathedral has always been important to me because it is a cathedral for our time which served as a meeting and assembly place. The Nana-cathedral became the world's most infamous 'whore' by receiving some 100,000 visitors during a relatively short three month exhibition which became in turn a festival and then a ceremony. The most important people to me are the creators of Bomarzo, the Spanish architect Gaudí, and the wonder-workers who erected the medieval cathedrals of Europe. I was not trained in an art school. I appreciate cathedrals because of their completeness; they represent more than a mere bit of an artist's creation for they are an entire *œuvre*. A residence can also become the complete expression of all that an artist can create; he can do anything and produce an integral and coherent work. Art is now confined almost exclusively to galleries and there are too few creative follies. When they are presented in a gallery, they become little more than an affront to the bourgeoisie. I do not create for galleries."

Returning to one of her most significant works, Niki describes the Stockholm Nana as "a cathedral for everyone. It was a pagan temple, and not a gallery object destined for the bourgeoisie, and was filled with objects and environments made specifically for the use of the people passing through. In the upper chambers there was a terrace and a dairy bar.

"Cathedrals were originally a meeting place for people. To their eyes the frescoes were the equivalent of today's comic strips—a pic-

220

torial text understood at a glance. One arm of the Nana-cathedral housed a small cinema where Greta Garbo's first film was shown. In another area there was a telephone linked directly to downtown Stockholm. In one knee children found a toboggan slide. The other leg contained a lovers' bench covered with red velvet. The lovers' conversations were transmitted to a loud speaker in the Nana's head. Synchronized with these transmissions, images of their faces were projected onto a screen in another section of the Nana. This was a modern cathedral for people.

"The Stockholm cathedral represented a return to the idea of a goddess of fertility. The body was entered through the birth canal. Tinguely constructed a machine to crush the bottles distributed by a Coca-Cola machine. There were objects from everyday life and objects from the fantastic side of life. This was a cathedral for mankind, partaking of the ordinary and the fantastic, a cathedral for a new era. I must say that Tinguely was of great help to me. Above all, he taught me that the dream is all and that technique is nothing. At first, I made bas-relief sculptures of Nanas that smiled and seemed to live, but which were usually plagued by a troublesome frozen appearance. I always wanted to see them step away from the wall and grow but I was unable to realize this wish. Tinguely told me: 'If you want to make them, do so; you can... Yes, it's the dream that counts,

not the technique which will always work itself out!' "

Niki de Saint-Phalle recalls that, when she and Tinguely arrived in Stockholm to construct the famous Nana-cathedral with Pontus Hultea and Ultvedt, none of them had a definite idea of what they would each create. Niki de Saint-Phalle and Tinguely first planned an "opera" or mechanical theater which would have one room and twelve stations each with three mechanical tableaux depicting "Woman Taking Control," "The Pope in New York" and other subjects. Niki wanted to make the woman, Tinguely to give it life, and Ultvedt to construct a reclining man in front of the woman. Their discussions continued and it was decided that Niki would begin her female figure. The group's enthusiasm for this project soon waned and they each began inspecting the chairs and tables of the Stockholm Museum in which they were working. The group almost lost all hope and Tinguely even proposed that they leave to spend a few days in Leningrad. Finally, they returned to their previous plans and decided to baptize this giant woman Hon or She. They procured chicken wire for the construction of the legs, had glue and colored pigments brought to them, and then began to build.

Ideas for the interior gradually took shape. There would be a bar, an exhibition chamber, a cinema. Then they ordered more than 750 yards of cloth. Ultvedt said, "Niki knew

France

immediately what colors she wanted to use and painted with absolute conviction and certainty."

Once the ventilation problems were solved, they began to paint the legs white. They finally used more than 240 pounds of carbon black. Tinguely built a "Radio Stockholm" similar to the radio sculptures he had been making since 1962. Niki de Saint-Phalle painted the cinema, the left arm, and then the colored streamer-tattoos. Ultvedt contrived new machines. Tinguely wanted to install a planetarium in the dome of the right breast of the giant woman. There was an artificial Milky Way made of lights. They eventually thought of the lovers' bench and of recording and broadcasting the conversations held there.

Ultvedt set to work painting the canvases to be displayed in the "gallery of fakes": a "Hourlouppe" by Dubuffet, a Fautrier, a Klee, a Pollock, and a Soulages—on each canvas a signature with one small but betraying mistake.

Work on the cinema and "emergency exit," both made by Gaston Wibom, was soon completed. Uniforms for the hostesses of Hon were also selected. Niki began to repaint the head while Tinguely created his "bottle crusher" for the bar thus eliminating the problem of discarded bottles. The entry passage and floor were covered with carpeting. Behind the lovers' bench they hung reproductions of paintings from the Modern Museum—an Yves Klein, "Shroud" by Kandinsky (1908), Léger's "Stair-

way" and a double portrait of Lucian Freud and Frank Auerbach by Francis Bacon. A telephone was installed in a globular plastic booth.

Hon was then ready to receive her "visitors." Her success was as great as her size. "I am cultivating delusions of grandeur," says Niki, "to prove that a 'silly woman' can create the most important objects of her era."

Niki smiles as she makes this statement, not because of that dream, but because of her dream of never sacrificing anything. "No; I am not rejecting one bit of my feminity; I love dresses and hats and making myself attractive. No; I do not want to give anything up. I want to add everything possible. Objects change and so also do my creations. My houses for Rainer are incomplete and will continue to develop. They are one thing among many and are always 'becoming' or transforming themselves as plans or as realities. Tinguely and I have now decided to create a 'monster head' that will be a den of pleasure as well as a cathedral for our era. We want to join with many artists in order to make this project a truly collective effort. We have already bought the land and will soon begin work. There will always be additions and refinements for this new project as there have been, and will continue to be, for Rainer's houses. My first Nanas were frozen, bas-relief figures which I shot at with paint pistols. They subsequently became joyful, independent women with power.

222

"The Bird's Dream is made to be lived in. It will never equal Bomarzo... The cathedral is a mythological woman rivaling Bomarzo. My greatest project is yet to be realized.

"The houses serve as a place for the founding and production of creations which will eventually blossom into still other forms."

The Bird's Dream is thus, for Niki de Saint-Phalle and for Rainer von Diez, a sketchy representation of one dream, among others, still incompletely formulated and waiting to be realized. What appears to be folly and pretense is actually the will to introduce into a reality, which both refuse to name, dreams which once given form and clarified also belong to the realm of creation. Sometimes when intellectually explaining an idea, Niki adds, "I must not say that or write that! It might be considered intelligent." Perhaps we should not try to explain dreams, but just acknowledge and transmit them. The surrealists accepted all expressions of the unconscious and were the first to save from oblivion such dream palaces as Bomarzo, and the houses and cathedral in Barcelona designed by Gaudí. The new realists, originally including Niki de Saint-Phalle, Yves Klein and Jean Tinguely, made reality participate in dreams. Ordinary objects, diverted from their usual functions, became real objects which were then transformed into dream elements.

The Bird's Dream is a reality, or rather a dream, which must be accepted as one entity containing other entities and still more dreams. These inhabitable sculptures are ultimately only different aspects of fragmentary and symbolic dreams: to sleep, to eat, to live in the sun, to live in shadow and darkness, and to plan and work on a dream which will always be unfinished. Everything could have been different and everything may still be different.

Ultimately it is of little importance to Niki de Saint-Phalle and Rainer von Diez that this residence is still incomplete and that it appears so, for a dream is but an outline of something to be developed and completed things are but the sketch of things yet to be created. Over the past few years the houses of the Bird's Dream have gone through a process of transformation. Niki's sculptures have been painted and in some cases modified. Various figures, the foliage and the dragon on the kitchen house, have been painted red, green, and black and the background has been covered with silver paint generally used to paint stoves. An area which was to serve as a sitting corner and in which they had initially planned to hang framed portraits of ancestors has become a troglodytic dining room and the table, bench, and silver ceiling are derived from this. The façade is made of polyester; the interior is modern and contains a table, a few chairs, a kitchen range, and an oven. The bedroom house is no longer set, as originally planned,

France

in a spider's body but in a giant polychrome Nana whose belly has two doors and whose chest has two round windows. On the ground floor is a bedroom. The floor of the bathroom is hollowed out in the form of a reclining Nana whose legs and arms are spread out to form a bathtub which one day may be reflected in pieces of mirror set in the walls. The giant head has also been painted silver. The three larger sculptures were to have been surrounded by satellite sculptures—animals and couples— grouped around a table, but Rainer von Diez suddenly feared that he would become, like his forebears whose life he has rejected, the curator of a museumlike residence which would have to be watched over like an object of art. The Bird's Dream must always remain a place where one comes to forget others.

Preceding page and opposite:
197-198. *In southern France, Niki de Saint-Phalle sculpts one by one the separate houses of the Bird's Dream for her friend Rainer von Diez, author of* The Long Wedding Night; General Prick, *performed in Munich; and, in collaboration with Niki de Saint-Phalle,* Ich (Me). *"One day I wanted to build something. I was in southern France; I liked those hills; I wanted to build something like a dream, a paradise in a forest; and that is how the Bird's Dream was born."*

199

200

200. *The Nana which replaced the traditional Greek temple as decor in* Lysistrata, *staged by Rainer von Diez in Munich.*

199. *Niki de Saint-Phalle's Nana for the Stockholm Exposition.*

201. *Rainer von Diez.*

201

202. *The kitchen-house. On the right, a Nana with a shopping bag. Near her, a polyester chair. On the door, a spider in the middle of foliage. On the left, on a wall overlooking the hills, an immense dragon above a heart. Under the window, a real table, glass, fork and spoon in a mass of polyester. To the right of the window and enveloped by the dragon, a couple in bed with sheets and blankets. On the roof, a bird. "On the wall not shown in the photo," says Niki de Saint-Phalle, "a bedroom will be outlined. The wall will be papered with striped wallpaper embroidered with real flowers pressed in plastic. People made of polyester will be seated on real chairs glued to the façade. In front of them will be a table and wicker chairs for Rainer's friends." The myths of the past will be no more legendary than the dragons and foliage of this dream.*

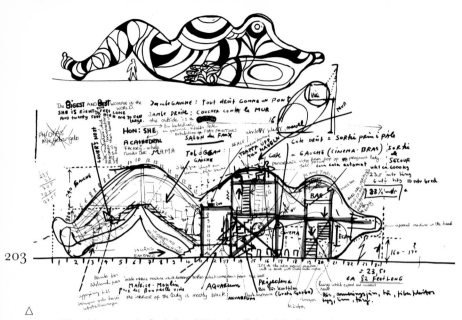

203. *The Nana-cathedral by Niki de Saint-Phalle and Jean Tinguely for the Stockholm Exposition.*

204. *One of the Nanas for the Bird's Dream. The Nana is saying: "I am the Nana dream house. Inside of me you can put anything you wish—a bar, a bed, a library, a bordel, a chapel. I am an adult's doll house—a refuge for dreaming."*

206. *This white, bald figure set among trees will eventually be painted and polyester hair transplanted on its head. Like small sheds found at the back of country gardens, this giant figure will serve as the toilet.*

205. *Model for Rainer von Diez's sphinx-house, used as the living room. The sphinx must be lived in, not questioned.*

Versailles

Versailles, a palace that contributed to the unity of France. The Grand Trianon, the most often plagiarized architectural folly of Europe. The Petit Trianon, built in an effort to forget Versailles. The Hamlet, where the Queen of France played the simple life.

Versailles Vanished

In a volume on follies, one chapter must be devoted to the immense folly and onerous stone dream with which Louis XIV of France burdened the Bourbon monarchy. Versailles was not only a folly economically, socially, politically and, sometimes, even aesthetically but it was also a folly because of its irrational inspiration—the Italian and magical atmosphere in which the French court lived with its spirit at once impregnated in the academic literary myths of the Ancient World and dazzled by illuminism, astrology, and mystico-Christian visions. Louis XIV, the Very Catholic King, the Lieutenant of Christ, the Lord's Anointed (he believed himself superior to the Pope, the product of a mere election), the Divine Light, and the Sun King—all these exaltations, all these deifications of one man who pretended to incarnate them all in his single person and alone be one people, all peoples, humanity, the entire universe and all that chaos which architects tried to control and impose on space—is

a brother in spirit of the individual who inspired Nietzsche in search of a superman. As Jean de La Bruyère said: "That is not healthy or reasonable." Louis de Saint-Simon wrote in other terms: "The King liked and counted only on himself and was his own resource in the final analysis."

The Versailles which can be seen today is a skeleton of Versailles in its royal splendor. We must remember that it is often impossible to identify the present rooms of the palace with those inhabited by the Sun King and important people of the court. The palace is the product of successive architectural plans. The original château was built (1624-61) under Louis XIII, with three major revisions later under Louis XIV: in 1661-68 by Louis Le Vau, in 1668-78 by François d'Orbay, and in 1678-1714 by Jules Hardouin-Mansart.

The present gardens, like the Château, provide only an idea of what they once were. Actually the baroque aspect of Versailles was more

233

207. The Dragon's Fountain, painting by Jean Cotelle. The greatest French architectural folly was Versailles. Unlike other follies built to escape reality, Versailles was motivated by a sense of actuality. Louis XIV believed that the only way to maintain power over the nobility, whose strength often exceeded his own, was not to fight but rather to captivate them and create the decor for sumptuous entertainment.

France

evident in the gardens than in the Château itself. French classicism may, indeed, be a more severe, more sober form of European baroque. Today we tend to judge works according to what remains of the original, isolated from the forces which gave them life and for which they were conceived, a kind of theater without scenery and actors or a palace without its fêtes. Yet such exteriors and surroundings, even if we merely begin to retrace their metamorphoses, indicate that architects were attracted to baroque. We need only to compare Mansart's château—constructed after 1678—with the former château of 1661 which enclosed the narrow marble courtyard on three sides, still similar to the interior courtyards of the Renaissance, in order to understand the movement which gave wings to former chrysalides, unfolding the structures to the natural surroundings rather than curling them up within the closed walls of a fortress. The Château de Versailles with its expansive façade, innumerable bays opening onto gardens and walks, suites of ceremonial halls and its monumental staircases, is baroque in conception despite the presence of its rectilinear walls. It is the gardens, however, because of their more apparent intricacies and their more immediate ties to the world of the fête, which undeniably constitute, along with the "follies" established at secret places for more intimate diversions, the most conclusive evidence of Versailles baroque.

In spite of a certain amount of destruction and remodeling, these gardens are still marked by a contradiction inherent to all that is baroque —the union of simplicity and diversity, of stasis and movement. Although geometry, perhaps severe and disfiguring for nature seemingly shaped and trimmed according to the dictates of straight cords and pruning tools, and simple patterns, often circles and squares which were essential elements of design *à la française*, did not completely determine the concept of the gardens or lead to an aesthetic formula, the gardens at Versailles merely reveal the function or role of gardens in a larger, synthetic entity —the royal castle as a center of power and pleasure. They were only the outer framework for the ever-changing spectacle of court life. These gardens were like fixed scenery which could be transformed for each fête, like a theater stage, and whose disposition facilitated the comings and goings of the spectators and enhanced the view in every direction with the help of long, rectilinear vistas and circles where walks intersected and radiated. This apparently simple geometry was the integrating framework of an immense stage of stone and greenery which was always prepared for the arrival of actors at each of the fêtes and which was animated on ordinary days by sculpture, fountains and a bustling crowd of courtiers.

Some of the most baroque aspects of these gardens have now vanished and only engravings show us the splendor of the gardens, especially the fountains, a characteristic feature of eighteenth-century decorative art, which are Arabic in origin rather than Italian, as generally believed.

The Grotto of Thetis, now gone but long considered the jewel of Versailles, was originally designed to raise the storage level of water to feed the fountains. A reservoir with a capacity of 570 cubic meters was fed by two pumps which brought water from a pond in Clagny to a level sixty-six feet above the terrace fountains. It was decorated with real shells, porcelain stalactites, mother-of-pearl, and mechanical birds whose wings flapped (such machines were fashionable at the time).

One of the peculiarities of Louis XIV and his contemporaries was a taste for practical jokes; and such a prank was installed in the Grotto of Thetis. Ladies of the court unaware of this trap were invited to visit the grotto; and, as they admired it, displaying the exaggerated wonder which court convention demanded, the king would make a sign and thin jets of water would spout from between the paving slabs, drenching them from below. Shrieks and laughter followed. Later, when the king grew older, such pranks were abandoned.

It is interesting to note, as did Bernard Teyssèdre, that the grotto, which was at first merely a pleasant addition to the gardens and a place for the young king to relax, was a secluded site where the cult of the Sun King began. Entering the grotto through a triple doorway, one passed between thick pillars which supported the reservoir. Niches had been carved into the back wall which once was decorated with figures evoking sea gods only to be abruptly transformed, in 1666, to create a space for the figures of sun horses and an Apollo surrounded by the Muses. Louis XIV liked to compare himself to the Apollo of the grotto being greeted by Thetis, sculpted after the Marquise de Montespan, the royal favorite at the time; and like Apollo he ruled over the world as well as his pleasure. At this time Versailles ceased to be merely a place of entertainment and became the center for the king's politics and the propagation of his policies. The fêtes were no longer only a pleasant means of diversion but also an occasion for the glorification of the king. Free access was replaced by strictly ceremonious processions and the improvised fêtes gave way to a kind of liturgy imposing the presence of the king. The former "pleasant additions" to the gardens became houses of worship or veneration and a visit to Versailles soon became a pilgrimage, revealing every step of the way the symbols of the omnipresence and the omnipotence of the God-King.

The fountains of the park required an elaborate system, and the quest for water at Versailles lasted almost as long as the palace was inhabited. In Louis XIV's time, water from the pond at Clagny had been diverted to the Grotto of Thetis, and the waters of the Bièvre River drained. Even the idea of bringing water from the Loire River to Versailles was contemplated, as later water was transported from the Juine River. Meanwhile the capacity of local ponds was increased. An adequate supply was not approached until the construction between 1675 and 1681 of the Machine de Marly at Louveciennes on an arm of the Seine. This operated sixty-four pumps, and even this did not obviate the need for new reservoirs and aqueducts and the exploitation of new sources. Even when it was working, not all the fountains could play at the same time.

Lavishness was typical of the seventeenth century. Despite material difficulties, many fountains were built—the Dragon's Fountain; Neptune's Fountain, which was not completed until Louis XV's reign; the Fountain of the Pyramid and the Fountain of the Cascade; and the Water Alley, designed by Claude Perrault, architect of the Louvre's colonnade, and named after the fourteen fountains which adorn it, seven on each side, with their white marble pools from which rise groups of children holding bowls of red Languedoc marble. At the beginning of the Pyramid Avenue are three tiers of pools, the water falling from one into the other; and, farther on, is the Cascade, or Nymphs' Bath, enhanced by a delightful group of nude statues by François Girardon.

The Fountain of the Pavilion and the Water Cradle were special attractions at Versailles. The Water Cradle consisted of a sloping path lined with curved jets of water so well directed that one could walk beneath them without getting wet. This was Spanish in taste, in accordance with the contemporary craze of the court, an echo of Hispano-Moorish patios, indifferent to the harsh winters which assailed Versailles and froze fountains and canals. The Water Cradle was later destroyed to make way for three fountains.

Returning toward the Royal Avenue and the Grove of the Bath of Apollo, royal guests would encounter a metal oak-tree with tin-plate leaves dispensing a spray of water—an idea of Mme de Maintenon, the mistress of Louis XIV who became his second wife. In the opposite direction, other jets sprang from the metal reeds of the pool. Not far distant, in a fountain, an eternal meal was served on dishes bathed in running water.

The Water Theater, of which only the Round Bower remains, was begun in 1671 when d'Orbay was the chief architect. This fountain had ten possible combinations which changed the form, grouping, and force of the water every two minutes.

The Grove of the Star, which can still be seen, is a focal point of the park of Versailles, with radiating paths terminating in distant fountains. This was the site of the Water Mountain, a bell-shaped, glittering, and sparkling fountain.

The Banquet Hall was replaced in 1706 by the present Fountain of the Obelisk, the work of Mansart, as were the canopies, resting spots, and rain shelters. These were completed by André Le Nôtre and are only known to us today from engravings.

The once gilded Fountain of Enceladus is still visible. Mlle de Scudéry stated in her *Promenades à Versailles* that she was charmed by this fountain, in which, she wrote, "gold and green look so well together." According to mythology, one of the giant sons of Tartarus and Earth, Enceladus, revolted against the gods and was crushed flat by lightning. Virgil consigned him to the bowels of Mount Etna, where his writhing causes earthquakes and his breath belches fire from the crater. The Versailles Enceladus combines the two legends and shows us a gigantic muscular form crushed beneath blocks of stone while—water replacing fire—Enceladus belches a jet 82 feet high, a feat which Louis XIV allegedly admired.

Next comes the Fountain of Apollo, designed by Charles Le Brun and representing Apollo on his chariot surrounded by four gilded tritons. Proceeding south toward the Château through the groves, we arrive at Mansart's celebrated colonnade, a series of arches made of pink Languedoc marble. In the past, the fountains played from 8 A.M. to 10 P.M. and poured water into the basin around Girardon's *Rape of Proserpina*.

The Chamber of the Horse Chestnuts, dating from 1704, recalls the French love of chestnut trees, the first of which was brought from Constantinople (and not India) and planted at the Hôtel de Soubise in Paris in 1615. This was the site of the Royal Island which has disappeared. However, the famous Queen's Grove still exists. Here on a warm July night in 1784 Jeanne de la Motte posed as Marie Antoinette (or, according to some, used a servant for the purpose) and duped the Cardinal de Rohan in the principal scene of the Affair of the Diamond Necklace. This famous episode caused a scandal on the eve of the Revolution and made the queen appear frivolous. Jewelers had completed an exorbitantly expensive necklace with several strands of diamonds for Mme du Barry just as Louis XV died. They proposed the necklace to Louis XVI who wanted to give it to the queen in 1778 after the birth of their daughter, Marie Thérèse Charlotte, but the queen refused because of the state of finances at the time and advised her husband to use the money instead to buy a ship. The situation was catastrophic for the jewelers. After a second refusal by the queen, the jeweler Boehmer called on the services of an adventuress, Mme de la Motte, who managed to slip into the queen's entourage.

The scandal involved another, much

more naïve, adventurer, Cardinal de Rohan who dreamed of replacing the Prime Minister Calonne. Mme de la Motte led him to believe that she could obtain the queen's aid for his project. And to better convince him that an exceptional gift for the queen would advance his plans, she promised him a meeting with Marie Antoinette. And one night in the Queen's Grove the cardinal was handed a rose by a white, regal silhouette who disappeared without saying a word.

After this meeting at the suggestion of Mme de la Motte, Cardinal de Rohan paid the jeweler a part of the price of the necklace; for the rest Mme de la Motte showed him a promissory note with Marie Antoinette's signature. The note was false. However, the exact role of the queen in this affair was never determined. When Boehmer applied to Marie Antoinette and to Breteuil, the Minister, who informed the king, a trial was held and the cardinal was sent to the Bastille. Mme de la Motte was branded and interned in the Salpêtrière, then a prison for women in Paris. The cardinal's cause was championed by the people of Paris, who were hostile to the queen, and Rohan, released from prison, was banished to his abbey.

Before its destiny as the scene of this notorious intrigue, the Queen's Grove contained a maze designed by Le Nôtre and adorned with thirty-nine fountains, representing Aesop's fables, which were made fashionable by La Fontaine.

The Parterre of Latona, named for Apollo's mother, was decorated with three ponds containing tortoises, reptiles, and, a special attraction, lead frogs which croaked as water poured from their mouths. Louis XIV, who had written a guide for visitors, pointed out the interest of this site.

The king loved orange trees, wanted them everywhere, and had them placed in silver tubs to decorate the state apartments. In 1768 Mansart was ordered to replace Louis Le Vau's Orangery and, in order to provide a more agreeable view, to make even bigger the large pond which had been built by a regiment of the Swiss Guards. Two flights of a hundred steps enhanced the majesty of Mansart's Orangery.

In Louis XIV's time the Fountain of Neptune had three pools, two of which were round. Its present form dates from Louis XV; and since 1785 it has consisted of one hundred and nine jets.

The Grand Canal, a Roman-inspired work which looks like a mirror at the end of the park, was animated in the seventeenth century by a small fleet of ships from Rouen, including a two-masted galley, as well as by English yachts, craft from the Levant, lateen-sail frigates, and magnificent Venetian feluccas and gondolas decorated with gold, mirrors, and brocade. The latter had been brought by gondoliers in black velvet jackets and bonnets, who founded a Venetian colony in Versailles, the descendants of which can still be seen today. The flotilla on the Grand Canal eventually became so big that it was placed under the control of the Naval Ministry, which provided crews wearing blue and red uniforms, their hair knotted with a ribbon. The adjacent royal vegetable garden also became so big that it was turned into the School of Horticulture.

The Château de Versailles rapidly became a town. The entire administrative apparatus of France was located there as well as the court. This meant new construction on the palace, of which Mansart was the architect. Mansart designed a new projecting façade of the Grand Gallery or Gallery of Mirrors. To house officials and offices, he joined the pavilions of Le Vau, forming the Ministers' Wings, and added the Grand Commun which housed the royal kitchens and contained lodgings for the cooks and their helpers, and became a barracks housing between 1,500 and 3,000 people.

It is perhaps surprising to note that there was no dining room in the Château de Versailles. The king always had his breakfast alone in his bedroom on a little table placed before the central window and generally took his other meals in one of the adjoining rooms, which was chosen according to the number of guests invited.

The Great and Small Stables, begun by Mansart in 1679, face the Château. Their two monumental entrances are decorated with equestrian high reliefs by Jean Raon and Pierre Granier. Under Louis XIV, the Mastership of the Horse was a much envied appointment because of the financial benefits to be gained (Saint-Simon's father had occupied the post). The significance of the post is symbolized by the fact that, at the death of the king, the Master of the Horse threw his sword into the burial vault.

It is almost impossible to identify the successive occupants of the many apartments in the Château. We know, however, that during Mansart's period the South Wing was occupied by the Dowager Princesse de Condé, the Duc du Maine, Mademoiselle, as the Duchesse de Montpensier was called, the Princesse Palatine, and the Duc d'Enghien. These suites had views on the gardens. The North Wing housed the Duc d'Orléans, the Duc de Chartres, the Prince de Conti, and the Dowager Princesse de Conti, daughter of Mlle de la Vallière, Louis XIV's first mistress.

The Small Apartments, or private apartments of the king, were located on the south side of the former small château of Louis XIII and faced the Marble Court.

Next to the Council Chamber was the Closet of Wigs. Louis XIV was bald and he constantly changed his wig (ceremonial wig,

239

morning wig, afternoon wig, hunting wig, etc.).

After the Closet of Wigs came the Closet of the Hounds. The king enjoyed feeding his hunting dogs, although the ventilation in this room seems to have been quite bad. Next came the Billiard Room, in which the king, reputedly an expert at the game, played every evening. It was followed by the Closet of Agates and Jewels, the remaining treasures of which are now shown in the Louvre's Apollo Gallery. This room was furnished with cabinets by André Charles Boulle. A small gallery led from it to the Closet of Medals, an octagonal room decorated with vases, ewers, and urns placed in fifty niches (most of these pieces are now in the National Library in Paris). Next to this was the Closet of Books, a modest library, the contents of which are now in the National Library. The Queen's Bedroom was at the far end of the Gallery of Mirrors; and Mme de Maintenon's suite of two rooms occupied the gallery built to connect the Louis XIII wing and the old dependencies. It was above the peristyle leading to the marble staircase, a noisy, drafty location. Mme de Maintenon's windows faced the Small Apartments of the king.

The State Apartments consisted of the Chamber of Venus, the Chamber of Diana, the Chamber of Mars (a concert room), the Chamber of Mercury, the Chamber of Apollo (the throne room), the Chamber of War, the Gallery of Mirrors and the Chamber of Peace.

The king went through these rooms on his way to mass every day.

The Gallery of Mirrors, the masterpiece of the aged Charles Le Brun (over sixty) and the young Jules Hardouin-Mansart (thirty-two), is the personification of Versailles lyricism and Italian grandiloquence. The contemporary visitor wishing to revive the vanished glories of the Gallery of Mirrors must imagine it furnished with silver tubs of orange trees, silver tables, more than forty chandeliers and candelabra, white damask curtains embroidered with the royal monogram in gold, Savonnerie carpets, all bathed in the dazzling brilliance of three thousand candles reflected in the tall mirrors.

Except for the walls, little remains of the décor which the great and privileged actually saw. Only three pieces of furniture remain of the myriad pieces at which Louis XIV once looked. Two are Mazarin chests, once in Cardinal Mazarin's library, and then in the king's bedroom at the Grand Trianon. The third is a clock by Boulle. Among other original objects now at Versailles are the statues in the Gallery of Mirrors and a few paintings, the most important of which is Veronese's *Feast in the House of Simon the Pharisee*, now in the Chamber of Hercules, designed by Robert de Cotte especially for this picture. The ceiling by François Lemoyne was also designed around Veronese's painting. From the Revolution until only a few years ago, this canvas was in the Louvre.

If he were to return to Versailles today, Louis XV might feel more at home than his great-grandfather since he would probably recognize his study with the famous desk designed by Jean François Oeben and completed by Jean Henri Riesener, which the Revolutionaries found too heavy to remove. Later it was transported to Paris; the Duc d'Orléans used it in Louis-Philippe's reign and next it was used by Napoleon III. The Wallace Collection in London has a copy, and copies were made for the King of Egypt and a Russian grand duke. It passed next to the National Furniture Depot and eventually came to the Louvre, from which it has been returned to Versailles. Would Louis XV also recognize his medal cabinet and two corner pieces made specially for the room? The clock on the mantelpiece used to strike for him. and there are six chairs on which Mme de Pompadour may have sat.

The park at Versailles, the trees of which were already old, was completely replanted in 1775 by Comte d'Angivilliers, director of the King's Buildings. During the early years of Louis XVI's reign when "English" gardens were fashionable, Versailles suffered the effects of this infatuation. Despite this, the work of Mansart and Le Nôtre was respected.

The Grand Trianon

At Versailles both the Grand Trianon, or Marble Trianon, built by Jules Hardouin-Mansart in 1687 at the order of Louis XIV, and the Petit Trianon, built by Jacques Ange Gabriel in 1755 for Louis XV, are open to the public.

The second may be preferred for its pure architecture and decoration and for the charm of the historical figures haunting it—Louis XV, Mme du Barry, and Marie Antoinette. Nonetheless, in its day, Louis XIV's Marble Trianon was an innovation and greatly influenced seventeenth-century princely residences. This was true to such a point that any edifice built at the extremity of a park was called a Trianon.

Trianon, the name of a village incorporated in the grounds of the Château de Versailles in 1661, was the site on which in 1670 Louis XIV commissioned Louis Le Vau to build a "house of porcelain for collations," as Saint-Simon described the pavilion known as the Porcelain Trianon because its façade was covered with blue and white faïence in the then emerging Chinese taste.

Louis XIV, however, did not like this Chinese fashion but preferred the Italian style and, during the summer of 1687, asked Mansart to replace the Chinese pavilion with "a

241

France

palace of marble, jasper, and porphyry, with delightful gardens" (Saint-Simon), which would include—Louis XIV insisted—a marble peristyle. Mansart asked Robert de Cotte to design the peristyle which connects the two wings of the palace. Mansart himself designed the rest of the Trianon, a one-story palace surmounted by a balustrade concealing flat roofs. The gardens of the Porcelain Trianon among which the Marble Trianon was built were considered as important as the peristyle by the king. The real belles of the Trianon have always been the flowers.

The king considered the Trianon as a country house reserved for his family and intimate friends. Even the princes of the blood had no right of entry but had to "ask permission" when they wished to dine there. As a child, Louis XV is said to have been happier at the Trianon than anywhere else.

Louis XIV chose the five-room suite of the left wing as his royal apartment. He wanted the decoration of his study (the King's Closet, or the Closet of Mirrors) to imitate his Council Chamber at Versailles. His visits to the Trianon did not interfere with his work as a king or with his obligations as a Catholic although religious practice was kept inconspicuous. Once mass had been said, the double-doors would close on the tiny chancel which held the altar, and there was nothing to suggest that the vestibule, decorated with a frieze on which Pierre

Lepautre had alternated ears of corn with clusters of grapes, led into the chapel.

In 1700, the king had his bedroom enlarged by combining it with the adjoining vestibule. The new royal bedroom was embellished with Corinthian columns and wood paneling which can still be admired. This suite was subsequently occupied by the Grand Dauphin, Louis XIV's eldest son, Madame Mère, the mother of Napoleon, and the Empress Marie Louise.

As with the Château de Versailles, it is difficult to obtain an exact image of what the Trianon was like during Louis XIV's reign since the mists of history envelop it. Nevertheless, despite the alterations which transformed the former billiard room into a chapel or the onetime bedroom of Mme de Pompadour into Napoleon's map room, the quarters which have accommodated Mme de Maintenon, Mme de Pompadour, and Queen Victoria of England can still be identified.

In the Trianon gardens Louis XIV practiced the art of being a grandfather. He could be seen there walking through the flowers holding the hand of the Duchesse de Bourgogne, the favorite among all his grandchildren, to whom he could be royally hard on occasion. The king was displeased when she became pregnant. When a courtier ventured the opinion that she might not be able to bear more children, the king interrupted in a rage: "Why should I care? Doesn't she already have a daughter?" And remembering that the state of the duchess had prevented him from going to Marly: "I will not be impeded anymore in my trips."

This anecdote also reminds us that in his last years, Louis XIV seemed to lose his taste for the Trianon, which was, after all, an inconvenient place in which to live. He is said to have personally ordered Mansart to build a new château and chose a site in the middle of the woods between Saint-Germain and Louveciennes with a fine view and surrounded by gentle hills. Mansart designed a square pavilion, dedicated to Apollo, emblem of the king, with twelve smaller pavilions, six on each side, intended for ministers and favorites. This new residence was the Château de Marly, no longer extant.

For similar reasons of inconvenience, the Grand Trianon was forsaken by Louis XV and Louis XVI for the Petit Trianon. Even before the construction of the latter, Louis XV rarely stayed at the Grand Trianon. He went there occasionally with Mme du Barry, and like the Sun King admitted only his intimate friends. In the small room in which Napoleon made his dining room took place the supper which was extremely important for the history of ideas in France and at which Mme de Pompadour, the Duc de la Vallière, and a few friends of the royal family were present. A discussion began among the guests on what gunpowder, used so much in hunting and war, was made of... was it sulfur, coal, or saltpeter?... Mme de Pompadour consoled the guests on their ignorance by admitting that she didn't even know what rouge, which she used on her face, was made of. At that, the Duc de la Vallière remarked that it was really a pity that His Majesty had forbidden Diderot and d'Alembert's encyclopedic dictionaries. At this, the king sent three footmen to the Château for the seven enormous proscribed quarto volumes in which they sought the chapters on powder and rouge while Louis XV was read the article on the Rights of the Crown... When it was finished, the king looked at everyone and said: "Now then, I say that this interdiction be raised!"

Although Louis XV and Louis XVI did not like the Grand Trianon, this was not true of the man who considered himself the real heir of the Sun King, Napoleon. The Grand Trianon was one of his favorite residences. But the idea which the emperor had of himself obliged him to refurnish it.

The restoration, in the late 1960's, of the Trianon, now used by foreign heads of state on official visits to France, had therefore to take into account the elements found there, Louis XIV paneling and Napoleonic furniture. Some of the original paintings have been refound; and the gallery named after Jean Cotelle, who was commissioned by Louis XIV

France

to execute paintings, has been reconstituted.

The Chamber of the Princes with its mantelpiece decorated with war trophies, was the vestibule of Louis XIV's suite, the bedroom of which now contains the bed which Napoleon used in the Tuileries and in which Louis XVIII died. The paneling in the vestibule and the king's bedroom, combined into one room in 1700, is still that which was installed during Louis XIV's reign.

Until 1703 Louis XIV's Council Chamber was the present Closet of Mirrors. This room was used as a council chamber by Louis XVI and Louis Philippe.

The right wing of the Grand Trianon contains the reception rooms. Louis XIV's music room, with paneling decorated with lyres, became the Officers' drawing room under Napoleon I and the billiard room under Louis Philippe. The original gaming vestibule and Closet of Sleep were made into one by Louis Philippe

who used it as a family drawing room. The round tables in the room had numbered drawers; each princess had her own key to open one of them.

The Grand Trianon was an uncomfortable place. The lack of privacy and adequate service space was such that several buildings had to be built to house servants, horses, carriages and even the kitchens, which had originally been placed in the basement near the king's apartment.

Once grown up, Louis XV never recaptured the pleasure which he felt there as a child. He was interested mainly in the gardens, had a menagerie prepared, and designed a French garden, in which Jacques Ange Gabriel built a pavilion in anticipation of the Petit Trianon. Gabriel also designed for Louis XV a botanical garden with hothouses, in which Bernard de Jussieu, the famous French botanist, was to begin his research.

The Petit Trianon

Like Louis XIV, Louis XV recognized the discomfort of the Grand Trianon and commissioned Jacques Ange Gabriel to build a smaller, more comfortable pavilion not far from the celebrated gardens of the Grand Trianon. The Petit Trianon was created to please Mme de Pompadour but she died in 1764

before its completion and the king inaugurated it in 1770 with his new mistress Mme du Barry. He wanted to make it his country house, a place of fantasy, a "folly." Gabriel used all the resources of his art in concentrating the essential elements into a small space. The king's residence consisted of only ten rooms in addition to rooms for his suite. The service rooms were inadequate and highly inconvenient. Louis XV spent very little time in Gabriel's small château. The Petit Trianon still exudes the presence of Marie Antoinette, the mythology created by her tragic fate and the material and moral attitudes of her age rather than the memory of Mme du Barry.

Louis XVI gave Marie Antoinette the Petit Trianon, which his grandfather had left to go to his deathbed. "You love flowers," he said to her, "I have a bouquet to offer you—the Trianon."

The nineteen-year-old queen longed for a refuge away from the court and her duties. Music, the theater, the company of a few friends, and flowers were her pleasure; she liked to come and go without ceremony. "She would," wrote Mme Campan, the queen's maid and author of *Memoirs of the Private Life of Marie Antoinette*, "enter the drawing room without expecting the ladies to leave the piano or their needle work, or the men to stop their games of billiards or backgammon."

The château consists of a ground floor, a second floor with five windows, separated by Corinthian pilasters, and an attic. On the ground floor were a guard-room, a hall, and a billiard room. The queen's second-floor suite, which faced out onto the garden, consisted of a boudoir, bedroom, and dressing room. This floor is divided in such a way that the top

sections of the windows light the library as well as the rooms of the lady-in-waiting and the lady of the bedchamber. The attic has fifteen rooms, some of which were occupied by Mme Elisabeth, Louis XVI's sister, and the Duchesse de Polignac, a friend of the queen who became governess to the royal children in 1782. One apartment was assigned to Marie Antoinette's four-year-old daughter and another to Louis XVI, who never used it.

One of Marie Antoinette's pages recorded that her room was "furnished in muslin" and brightly colored embroidery and decorated with portraits of her brothers and sisters, as well as a view of Vienna and a small map of Austria. She preserved the paneling designed by Gabriel and executed by Guibert. For the rest, our imagination can be whetted by prints of the period and portraits by Mme Vigée-Lebrun of the queen described by the artist as "tall and admirably shaped, plump but not too plump... she walked better than any woman in France... her face had the long oval contour peculiar to the Austrian nation... her eyes were almost blue... her lips rather full." She also described her radiant complexion but did not mention that she had red hair. Mme du Barry called her the "small carrot."

The queen's boudoir, from which she could descend directly to the garden without passing through the drawing rooms, thus preserving her highly prized independence, was paneled.

France

A mechanism masked the windows with glass panels. A new white marble chimney-piece was installed. The wood paneling, attributed to Rousseau fils, was decorated with a flowered wreath, a dove flying away from a garland, a bow and arrow, perfume-braziers, amphora, cornucopias, genii, rose leaves, and in the middle the monogram M. A. The carving is infinitely fragile and delicate, almost too meticulous in its detail. The tiny room is furnished with a divan, three armchairs, and two other chairs.

The bane of existence at the Petit Trianon was the kitchen and pantries in the basement, which also contained the dumbwaiter for mounting ready-laid tables to the room where Louis XV and Mme du Barry used to dine. Marie Antoinette was bothered by the coal fumes and in 1781 the kitchen was transferred to annex buildings. In the dining room, the queen placed two large paintings which her mother, Empress Maria Theresa of Austria, sent from Vienna. One represents Marie Antoinette as a child, performing a ballet with her brothers for the wedding of her brother Joseph II. The two paintings still hang where the queen had them placed in 1778.

Marie Antoinette was not content with merely redecorating and refurnishing the Petit Trianon. At her orders, the architect Richard Mique built the Theater, the Temple of Love inside which is a copy of Bouchardon's statue of Love, the Concert Pavilion, and the cottages of the Queen's Hamlet. But her triumph was the gardens done by the Comte de Caraman, Mique, and the gardeners Claude Richard, père et fils. The queen arranged and planted these gardens which soon became the most famous of the period and, along with those at Ermenonville and Saint-Leu, served as a model for many others. King Gustavus Adolphus III of Sweden asked her for the plans during his visit to Paris in 1784. Nonetheless, these so-called "English" gardens, which eighteenth-century Englishmen referred to as "Chinese," were not new and had been fashionable in France since the end of Louis XV's reign, long before Rousseau's theories were known. Like all the artists and thinkers of his day, Rousseau believed that they indicated a return to nature and praised them accordingly.

The Petit Trianon thus became the special domain of Marie Antoinette. Her "trips" to the Petit Trianon, as the periods which she spent there were called, have left behind few traces for she maintained a mystery over her life in the small palace. This mystery has been much discussed, and the Temple of Love bears much of the responsibility for this. From 1779 to 1788, during which Marie Antoinette visited the Petit Trianon twice a year, in the spring and summer, many fêtes were held. On those warm evenings, the Temple of Love, near which Claude Richard had planted exotic trees, bushes of snow-white roses, and weeping willows, was etched against the sky in the light of hundreds of torches. Perhaps the Swedish

diplomat, Count Hans Axel von Fersen, whom the queen admired, was in attendance on some of those evenings.

The Hamlet

A few hundred yards from the Petit Trianon are nine thatched cottages comprising a village with a water-mill and diminutive gardens enclosed by simple fences. The grounds had orchards where apples, cherries, peaches, and apricots were cultivated. Red and black currants, roses, honeysuckle, and cauliflower were also grown. The Hamlet, a world of make-believe, was built by Richard Mique after relief models by Hubert Robert.

Hamlets were fashionable in the late eighteenth century. One had been built at Chantilly for the Prince de Condé, another at Raincy for the Duc d'Orléans, and still another with real cows, sheep, goats, and chickens at Montreuil for the Comtesse de Provence. The queen could not be without her Hamlet.

The first cottage encountered coming from the Petit Trianon is the Queen's Cottage. This is connected with the Billiard Cottage by a wooden gallery leading to a staircase built around a poplar tree. On the ground floor of the Queen's Cottage are a dining room and a backgammon room and on the second floor an antechamber and a small drawing room. The

rooms are now bare. In Marie Antoinette's day, the ceilings were white and the moldings and paneling white and gold. The queen probably came only for brief moments of leisure to these cottages which Napoleon's architect, who restored them, rudely described as "small trysting places."

Above the billiard room, a "Chinese" room recalls a different fashion which the period had inherited from Louis XV's reign. The taste for lacquered objects lasted until the Revolution. Lafont d'Ausonne, author of *Mémoires secrets*, tells how "after dinner, which occasionally took place in the mill but most often in the Queen's Cottage, we would dance a few country rounds to the light strains of a mandoline and a tambourine." The king sometimes took part in these dinners, as his diary records.

Marie Antoinette loved flowers, masses of flowers in pots of white Lorraine earthenware with her initials in blue surrounded by roses. In the spring of 1786, these pots contained double-flowered hyacinths, which lined the gallery and the steps of the stairway.

Just behind the Queen's Cottage is the

247

France

Réchauffoir (kitchen) where meals were prepared or merely reheated, as well as a small thatched cottage for the servants.

From her balcony, the queen of the Hamlet could survey her entire domain: the stream and the white lane separating it from the mill; the Boudoir, or Queen's Smaller Cottage, and its flight of nine stone steps; the Colombier, or Dovecote, with its aviary and poultry yard, the bowling alley with arches of climbing roses; and by the lake, among leaves and branches, Marlborough's Tower, named after an old ballad and used to store fishing tackle. Next to the tower is the Clean Dairy, or summer dining room, furnished with marble tables. Marie Antoinette was very fond of dairy products and such a glutton for "iced cream" that she made herself ill by eating too much of it. Across the lane stood the Preparation Dairy, which was demolished in 1810. Beyond was the farm, worked by a peasant family from Touraine, with a few sheep and goats, including a he-goat which "must be white and good-tempered," said the queen. This farm had only one horse, bought in October, 1789, after the royal family had been forced to leave Versailles. For a time it was used to carry butter and cream for them from the Hamlet to the Tuileries Palace in Paris. But, at that time, the queen was already far from "the light strains of the mandoline and the tambourine."

On October 5, 1789, the queen was in the grotto at the foot of the Montagne de l'Escargot (Snail Mountain), not far from the Belvédère. "The grotto is reached," wrote the Comte d'Hézecques, "by following a meandering stream. Its opening was so dark that my eyes needed time to become accustomed to the dark and begin to see objects... A bed of moss stretched out invitingly... a crack in the wall over the bed of moss opened onto a meadow and exposed in the distance anyone who would have liked to approach this mysterious retreat; a dark stairway led to the summit of the slope through a close thicket and screened from view any object which one might wish to hide."

The grotto was a refuge. What was Marie Antoinette doing there on that fateful autumn day? There, according to Mme Campan, a messenger sent from the Château warned her that the people of Paris were marching on Versailles. The queen rose at once and left the Petit Trianon, never to return.

208. The Theater of Water seen from the Amphitheater, *painting by Jean Cotelle.*

209. Grove of the Three Fountains, *by Jean Cotelle.*

210. Labyrinth, *by Etienne Allegrain.*

211. The Grand Trianon, *by Jean Cotelle.*

212. Labyrinth and the Grotto of Birds, *by Jean Cotelle.*

213. The Orangery and the Lake of the Swiss Guards, *by Jean Cotelle.*

214. Fountain of Neptune, *by J. B. Martin.*

215. The Grove, *by Jean Cotelle.*

216. Inside the Labyrinth, *by Jean Cotelle.*

217. *The Grotto of Thetis built in the park at Versailles by Louis XIV in 1679 for Mademoiselle de la Vallière.*

Next page:
219. *Marie Antoinette's Hamlet near the Petit Trianon serves as a reminder that the queen was Austrian. The thatched roofs, the mills, and the lake evoke the countryside around Vienna, not that around Paris.*

218. *Four masks in the Grotto of Thetis.* ▷

217

218

220. *One of the thatched cottages of the Hamlet.* 220

222

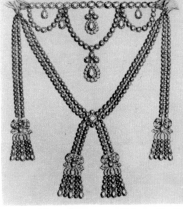

221. *Marie Antoinette at the Hamlet.*

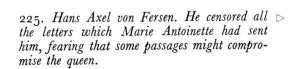

224

224. *The famous affair of the diamond necklace, a scandal which affected the queen, took place in the park at Versailles. The necklace disappeared on the eve of the Revolution.*

222-223. *Napoleon's architect, who restored these cottages, referred to them as "small trysting places." The queen received the Swedish diplomat Hans Axel von Fersen here under mysterious and romantic circumstances.*

225. *Hans Axel von Fersen. He censored all* ▷ *the letters which Marie Antoinette had sent him, fearing that some passages might compromise the queen.*

225

223

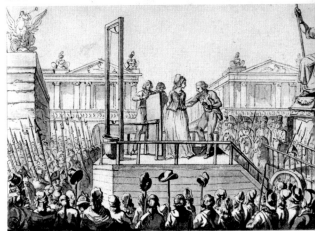

226

226. *Marie Antoinette on the scaffold.*

The Mystery of
the Monsters of Bomarzo

Prince Orsini's mysterious monsters were perhaps influenced by Ariosto.

Gigantic statues of monsters are found in the gardens of Bomarzo, called the Sacred Wood, around the Palazzo Orsini, near Viterbo, Italy. Although these figures have no apparent historical significance, they have inspired many legends. One alleges that Turks, captured at the Battle of Lepanto and brought to Bomarzo, carved them in 1571; another that one of the Orsini, the family that built the estate, tried to keep his wife by terrorizing her with the statues. They were commissioned by a nobleman, perhaps the man who had engraved on the upper lip of one of these ogres an inscription which André Pieyre de Mandiargues, the French poet and novelist, reads as: "*Ogni pensiero vole*," translated by him: "Every thought flies away." The originator of these wonders was probably more preoccupied with frivolities than with serious matters. However, it may also be a somewhat effaced reproduction of Dante's sentence: "*Lasciate ogni pensiero voi che entrate*" ("You who enter here, leave all hope behind"), which would make its meaning much more serious.

Here the horrible is so fantastic that it merges with the beautiful. The monsters and giants are similar to those found in passages from mannerist literature, such as Canto XI of Ariosto's *Orlando Furioso*, in which a giant slaughters travelers, skins, and rends them limb from limb, and then devours them, sucking their blood and brains and gnawing their flesh down to the bones which he scatters like trophies around his cave. In art the sixteenth-century Bomarzo is one of the most striking manifestations of the mannerist movement.

Near Viterbo, within two hours of Rome, one may find many palaces with curious sculptures. At one a stone ship supporting a child sails in the middle of a pool; at the Villa Lante the cascades are so constructed that the sound of the falling water creates an effect of surprise; and at the entrance to the palace of the Countess Cini, a basin carved with gigantic figures fantastically recalls the ancient Etruscans. But these sculptures do not exhibit the marked taste for the horrifying and the startling which characterizes Bomarzo. The odd-shaped stones found on its grounds may have conjured up such travesties in the sculptor's mind, or nature herself may have prompted the imagination of the lord of this domain. Whatever the reason, we know from contemporary correspondence between the Duke Orsini and a friend, who was a poet, that these sculptures were accepted in Renaissance society as wonders. Bomarzo should, therefore, be looked at as a "chamber of wonders," rather than as a "chamber of horrors." On one of the stones in the Orsini garden we can read: "You who wander across

257

227. *The cool chamber at Bomarzo is entered through the gaping mouth of a monster.*

the world, eager to see lofty and astounding wonders, come here and you will find terrifying faces, elephants, lions, bears, ogres, and dragons." On another: "If Rhodes is proud of its Colossus, I too have my little wood of Bomarzo, which merits no less pride." And on the base of a sphinx: "All thoughts be gone."

The prince thus wanted to astound just as the Ancients had done. He was a humanist as well, for these monsters reveal the man who conceived them and whose imagination was omnipresent. This man was Duke Pierfrancesco Vicino Orsini, heir to the feudal castle of the Orsini, in this province of Latium which contained so many princely villas. He transformed the family residence, probably with the aid of Giacomo da Vignola, the architect who had designed the Villa Caprarola for the Farnese family and, also in the neighborhood of Viterbo, the Villa Lante. But all this is uncertain. We know, however—from correspondence between the poet Annibale Caro and Duke Orsini—that the latter had commissioned frescoes depicting a battle of giants for the walls of the great house. Annibale advised him to approach a painter of the school of Zuccari to undertake the job. From one of Annibale's letters to Vicino Orsini, we may assume that work on the park of Bomarzo was begun around 1564 and that at this time the essentially mannerist theme of giants and monsters haunted the duke's mind. Annibale refers to the work engag-

ing him at Frascati, to the same extent perhaps as Orsini was absorbed by the theater and the mausoleums of Bomarzo. In another letter the poet apologizes "for being occupied no less than he by his wonders of Bomarzo." He approves the theme of the giants for the garden "where there are so many other extravagant and supernatural elements." Vicino Orsini did not, therefore, appear half-mad to a humanist of 1564, but rather as a man responsive to and deriving inspiration from the marvelous.

Living in the palazzo which dominates the woods at Bomarzo, where he walked every day, Orsini was at leisure to develop the layout of his park. He decided how best to use the sloping terrain and how to arrange the sculptured subjects in relation to the itinerary which one follows quite naturally today and which is also that of the stream that runs through.

The first sculpture encountered is that of a giant grasping the legs of a figure whose head hangs down. It has often been thought that this composition depicts one of the struggles of Hercules or a hero wrestling with a human figure. But the erosion of the victim's body precludes any certainty. The stream leads next to a giant tortoise placed upon a human statue with upraised arms. This is close to a tilted fountain, from which Pegasus rises on a jet from water seemingly not parallel with the ground. This gives the impression that the landscape has been shaken by an earthquake.

The Mystery of the Monsters of Bomarzo

We now come to a grotto, carved with three graces and three nymphs, followed by a platform with two sculptured nymphs and a two-story leaning house, engraved with the maxim: "Resting, the mind becomes wiser" ("*Anima quiescendo prudentior ergo*"). Further on we read on the pedestal of a female sphinx:

Chi con ciglia inarcarte
E labbra strette
Non va per questo loco
Manco ammira
Le famose del mondo
Moli sette.

which Germain Bazin translated as: "He who fails to pass through this place with eyes wide open and lips pressed shut will fail to admire the seven wonders of the world."

This palace, deliberately built on a slant, is a prelude to the follies to be built two hundred years later, houses set "in foliage," slightly foolish and always associated with a stream, a maxim, and a story. But here there is no story. Nearby, on the naturally formed terrace, there still lies a row of monstrous severed heads and upturned stone vases, attributed to various sculptors, including Bartolomeo Ammanati, but no document exists to prove it.

According to Maurizio Calvesi, the garden of Bomarzo offers analogies with the text of *Amadigi* (1560) by Bernardo Tasso and *Gerusalemme Liberata* by his son Torquato. We know that such literature influenced the nobility of the period and the artists to whom they entrusted the decoration of their palaces. Ascending once again the central terrace, we see the principal figures of Bomarzo amid the long grass: on a rockside, in the background, approached by a vase-lined path, an olympian Jupiter, or some barbarous figure akin to the god, a winged dragon attacked by mastiffs, a gigantic elephant saddled with a palanquin and pinning a Roman centurion on the ground with his trunk. Farther on, under the trees, opposite the god carved in the rock, a female figure supports on her head a stone amphora planted with cactuses, the back carved with two Tritons struggling with an upside-down human figure.

Above this terrace, if we go up the hill again, the figure of a woman can be seen under a blanket of moss, waiting for Jupiter transformed into golden rain. Near her a sea-dragon, with gaping jaws, emerges anachronistically from the earth.

A staircase mounts to the third platform, which dominates the valley and leads to a succession of strange figures, giant winged sirens and the heraldic bears of the Orsini, bearing on their arms roses.

Returning to the second platform, one is confronted below by the enormous mask head, its mouth agape, of the cool chamber where one may sit around a stone table. A similar

259

head guards the entrance to the house of the architect and painter Federico Zuccari in Rome, and two drawings of this motif are in the Vatican Library.

Retracing our steps toward the entrance of the wood of Bomarzo, we see on the right the round head of a monster with large teeth crowned by a stone sphere. Behind this head a stairway ascends to a large meadow with a small burial temple with Tuscan columns decorated with skulls and tibias, the only classical structure among the weird masonry and extraordinary sculpture.

The gardens of Bomarzo barely outlived their owner. Duke Vicino vanished about 1574. His illegitimate son, Leonida, whom he legitimatized in 1572, does not seem to have shared his father's tastes, nor did his descendants who, in 1645, sold the properties of Bomarzo and Chia for 185,000 scudi to Monsignor Ippolito

Lante della Rovere. Bomarzo was forgotten and run over by brambles.

When the dadaists and surrealists were rediscovering primitive art and the poetry of automatic writing, Bomarzo and the Desert of Retz, in France, were rescued by them from the neglect into which they had fallen. Creations of an imagination which gave expression to every whim through the style of a period, these monuments were for them manifestations of the unconscious and of the attitudes and tendencies of an age of which they saw themselves the heirs. André Breton, Jean Cocteau, Salvador Dali, and, later, André Pieyre de Mandiargues spoke of Bomarzo as of a place entirely exceptional. They admired through the surrealism of the figures and the pervasive symbolism of this curious garden what they appreciated elsewhere in primitive art, that is the primeval aspect of the symbolic.

228. *The head of a monster crowned with a sphere at the entrance to the garden at Bomarzo.*

231

231. *An elephant crushing a centurion.*

232. *One of many giant heads near the leaning house.*

232

233. *A siren with two tails.* ▷

Preceding pages:
229. *A winged siren. The tail and wing are more than
6 ¹/₂ feet long.*

230. *Battle of the Giants, perhaps inspired by Ariosto's
Orlando Furioso (11th Canto).*

233

234

234. *Heads attributed to Bartolomeo Ammanati.*

235

235. *Duke Vicino Orsini.*

236

236. *Rear view of the statue shown in Figure 237. Two winged sirens fight with a man.*

237. *Woman bearing an amphora on her head.* ▷

The Gardens of Caserta

A world of the baroque and of the natural.

The first impression one has of the eighteenth-century royal palace at Caserta near Naples is that of an almost excessive grandeur. The edifice forms a quadrilateral, each side of which is 835 feet long and the walls of which, worthy of the Escorial in Spain, are 132 feet high. Behind the palace stretches a two-mile vista running through a 240-acre park. Water, collected on Monte Taburo, originates in a distant stream, is brought to the gardens over a 25-mile long aqueduct, and falls 265 feet before arriving at the fountains of the castle. And this is only a small part of the complex conceived of by King Charles III of Naples. It has been said that his was a megalomaniacal dream but it must be considered in the context of the time. How many megalomaniacs were there in Enlightened Europe? The continent never saw as much construction on a grand scale as in the eighteenth century—Berlin, St. Petersburg, Vienna, Munich, Wurtzburg, etc. At Einsiedeln, the Esterhazys who were neither kings nor dukes nor prince-electors built a coffee house, an opera, and a theater for their castle.

In the eighteenth century, Naples was the third largest city of Europe after London and Paris and before Rome. In 1734, when Charles, son of Philip V of Spain and Elisabeth Farnese, and Duke of Parma since the death of Antonio Farnese, recaptured Naples from the Austrians, he was unaware of the fact that his capital was larger than Madrid. The new, young king, then only eighteen, felt that he had to assert his authority and he did so as all the sovereigns of his period against the cities which were becoming larger, richer, and stronger—through a close solidarity with a court, a government, and an administrative apparatus around him.

Like his contemporaries, the enlightened despots, Charles III wanted to be the protector of the arts and sciences and planned in his new royal city a public library, a university, and an observatory in addition to military barracks. Like Louis XIV, his great-grandfather, he gathered the strength and glory of the State around himself. This is one of the many similarities between Versailles and Caserta.

Caserta, once a very small town with a royal hunting lodge and woods like the Versailles of Louis XIII, tempted Charles, who was just as enthusiastic about hunting as Louis XIV had been. This trait was common to the Bourbons as was a taste for beautiful and noble buildings. However, such similarities, quite common from one king to another, should not be overemphasized. They simply explain, in part, the extreme taste found in the decoration of the castle's rooms—the Hall of the Halberdiers, the Hall of the Guards, or the Hall of Alexander—

238. *The Grande Cascade in the park at Caserta. Actaeon is pursued by Diana's hounds.*

in the pilasters on the walls and in the gilt on the ceiling and capitals. But no stairway at Versailles, except the Stairway of the Ambassadors, could be compared with the famous central "scalone" at Caserta, the masterpiece of Luigi Vanvitelli's plan. It forms a veritable marble cascade in the center of the castle. People have praised the classical lines of the façade, but they forget that it does not correspond exactly to Vanvitelli's project, that it lacks a dome in the center and towers at the angles.

Who was Luigi Vanvitelli? When Charles began to look for an architect around 1750, he found no one in Naples who could qualify for the project. The artistic capital of Italy was Rome. Nicola Salvi, the architect of the Fontana di Trevi in Rome, would have suited him, a revealing choice since it indicates that he was already thinking of the castle's garden. But Salvi was not available and he finally asked Vanvitelli who accepted the royal offer. Vanvitelli was the Italianized son of a Dutch painter, Van Vitel, and had been brought up in Naples before studying in Rome. By the time he was fifty, he had asserted his personality by transforming the interior of the church of Santa Maria degli Angeli in Rome, originally designed by Michelangelo, and had probably studied with Filippo Juvara, architect of the Superga basilica as well as the admirable Stupinigi palace near Turin. Vanvitelli, not a conventional architect, was notably versatile and talented; his work reflects his harmonious eclecticism at a turning point in the century the first half of which had seen rococo triumph in Germany, rocaille in France, Palladianism in England, and the most extravagant baroque in Spain. In Rome, which rebelled against rococo, the return to antiquity began near Naples with the excavation of Herculaneum and Pompeii, while farther south the doric temples of Paestum fascinated young artists from all of Europe. Caserta is the product of this diversity and Vanvitelli imposed on his baroque and academic colleagues, painters, and sculptors that *grandessa*, inherited from Rome rather than from France, which was able to control extremes of taste.

Charles of Bourbon was also hostile to extremes. What was his role in the preparation of the plans? This is difficult to determine but the king, conscientious, organized, prudent, and liking fêtes and spectacles, probably wanted to examine every detail. The realism of the statues in the park indicates a certain reserve and the choice of the fable of Diana and Actaeon as a theme may well have been intended as a moralizing gesture.

The dual construction of the park and the castle from 1752 to 1774 was to keep the architect busy until his death. Vanvitelli directed and coordinated the work and designed the general outline, but left his colleagues free to express their various talents inside the castle and in the layout of the park. The undertaking was so gigantic that its initiator did not live to see it completed. It was to be finished under other sovereigns—Ferdinando and Maria Carolina of Austria (1759-1806), Murat and Caroline Bonaparte (1808-15), Ferdinando and his second wife the Duchess of Floridia (1815-25) and then Francesco I. However, the times changed. The castle of Charles, the hunter, became the castle of more worldly affairs. The innumerable fêtes organized there spilled out of the royal theater and the long vista, and the succession of men and women made the castle, especially its park, the living conservatory of an end-of-the-century rich in metamorphosis.

Luigi Vanvitelli opened a long vista *à la française* running through the former woods of green oaks to the fountains supplied with water from the Tiburno. It took several years to build the immense aqueduct through the hills along with its tunnels and three viaducts, the longest of which, the Ponte della Valle, is three times as long as the Pont du Gard, the Roman aqueduct in southern France. In 1762 at a memorable ceremony, the water was channeled into pipes and four hours later, according to Vanvitelli's estimates, spilled forth with a loud roar across the rocks of the artificial cascade. The bounding water gradually slowed down as it descended from fountain to fountain. Similar sights could be seen in such Renais-

sance villas as the Villa d'Este and the Villa Torlonia. This surprising baroque efflorescence in the park at Caserta was nothing other than a return to Italian tradition.

Luigi Vanvitelli, who died in 1773, was succeeded by his son Carlo who had been his assistant. Carlo designed the plans of the fountain basins and their decorative elements and engaged the sculptors who had worked on the interior decoration of the castle to carve the mythological groups of the fountains—Angelo Brunelli, Gaetano Salmone, and the Solari brothers, all Neapolitans. The baroque spirit remained alive in these provincial artists, but in a country filled with the presence of antiquity and theatrical representations the heroes of mythology were quite unlike those hieratic or pompous figures found elsewhere at the top or in the center of fountains. The desire for the natural, evident in the statuary of the water theater, was similar to intimist preoccupations rampant in society at the end of the eighteenth century when Jean Jacques Rousseau preached a return to a simpler life.

At Caserta terraces and fountains succeed one another, charging up the hill as if in assault. The arrangement is just the opposite of that at Versailles, since at Caserta the ground rises from the castle toward the woods instead of sloping off toward distant hunting grounds. From level to level the scene changes. At the foot of the cascade are two groups of statues,

Italy

that of Diana and her servitors and that of Actaeon, the hunter metamorphosed into a stag and hunted by his own dogs. A staircase descends to a fountain where Venus is attempting to detain Adonis. On a lower level, an aerial Ceres dominates an agile group of young Nereids running about in search of water.

Lower down is the immense fountain of Eolus in which the water falls in long tresses from the top of a portico made of arcades and grottoes; then comes a bridge, the Brigde of Hercules, a long green rug at the end of which, after the Fountain of Marguerite, runs a silent and empty path between the trees and the castle. In this gigantic exposition of staircases and fountains, the baroque found one of its most moving and significant expressions. Water pours from stone dreams, a concept born from the primordial image of rushing water, creator of movement and form. The baroque found its Fountain of Youth at Caserta thanks to Vanvitelli's aqueduct.

Lower still along the vista a double row of clipped trees encloses larger trees. The paths of the parterre radiate out from a central design, but once at the park abandon their rectilinear pattern and, further on, turn back in front of the wild forest. This is the border between two worlds on which was built a miniature fortress, la Castelluccia, later a supposed refuge for lovers.

The botanical gardens, which the voyages of Wallis, Cook, and Bougainville had made fashionable, were not at all romantic. But gradually a change had occurred. At this particular moment amateur botanists began to dream of distant voyages to unknown countries where exotic plants flourished. Such plants had their own foreign character and transformed the landscape. Carlo Vanvitelli who worked on the garden with Graefer, the Irish naturalist, curiously built a portico in the gardens at Caserta. Was this a reminder of Herculaneum and Pompeii? Had he perceived the bond between exoticism and antiquity? The unknown places which the plants re-created, similar to time revived through ruins, transmitted a message—the revelation of another world which the baroque of palaces hid behind their elaborate décor. A simple passage separates the Fountain of Diana from the English garden, but in crossing it one passes from one world into another, from the world of fêtes to that of solitude. This moving transition is symbolized by a unique and lonely Venus, kneeling like an unknown divinity without any attributes but expressing nature seemingly rediscovered by her.

Next pages :
240. *Fountain of Diana.*

241. *Nymphs playing with cupids and a boar.*

242. *Fountain of the Dolphins.*

243. *Fountain of Actaeon.*

239. *A term against a wall of trees.* ▷

244

The Palace of Isola Bella

The Palazzo Borromeo is the architectural folly of an entire family rather than a single individual.

The palace of Isola Bella, as the name suggests, is set upon an island. It is a dream so extravagant that those who conceived it had been long dead by the time the structure was finished.

The Palazzo Borromeo on Isola Bella in Lake Maggiore in north Italy consumed the energy of several generations of the family after which it is named. Begun in 1630, it took three centuries to complete. From the opposite shore of Lake Maggiore it looks like a ship anchored in the middle of the lake, a reference perhaps to the legend that the Borromeo family is descended from pirates, although it includes bishops and a saint in its lineage.

The Palazzo Borromeo has remained in the Borromeo family to the present day. The Borromeos date back to Saint Justin, who was martyred under Diocletian in A.D. 303. According to legend, members of the Borromeo family sailed the seas under the skull and crossbones and the family inherited its fortune from a pirate. In any event, the fortune which built the architectural folly of Isola Bella existed under Vitaliano I in 1449. Most of Lake Maggiore belonged to the family at that time. Vitaliano VI, who died in 1690, played a major role in the completion of the palace.

Vitaliano Borromeo, grand-nephew of Saint Carlo Borromeo, wanted his palace to resemble a structure built on the prow of a ship. It features a stone wall raised above the water. The wall, which supports hanging gardens, is hollowed out in places to let in the sun, and to light a series of grottoes. Morelli was the first architect to submit plans for the palace to Vitaliano Borromeo but the Papal architect Carlo Fontana did most of the work and Barca designed the gardens.

The palace of Isola Bella and its gardens, completed in 1670, are not the dream of one man but of a family who chose the statues and contrived the enchanted atmosphere of the artificial grottoes over a period of three hundred years. However, the palazzo was never completely finished. The interior of the palace has high ceilings and the baroque ostentation of its decoration clashes with its romantic setting. From its windows can be seen the far shore of Lake Maggiore and the Isola dei Pescatori. Also in view are fishing boats drawn up on the beach of Isola Bella, whose owners occupy the village on the island. Although the palace and its grounds cover two-thirds of Isola Bella, the property of the Borromeo family has remained until now isolated from the modern world.

244. *A white peacock sits like an ornament on the hand of a statue in the gardens of the Palazzo Borromeo on Isola Bella in Lake Maggiore.*

Italy

Indeed, it will probably remain so because of its island situation.

This fabulous site of flowering lemon trees seemed an extraordinary place to Goethe as well as to Wagner, who stayed there after his romance with Mathilda Wesendonck. Describing Isola Bella in a letter to her, Wagner wrote from Venice: "As I already knew the island, I dismissed the gardener in order to be alone. It was a delightful summer day and suddenly I was once more serene and at peace, a feeling so wonderful that I knew it could not last." *Tristan and Isolde* was finished; Wagner was working on *Parsifal*, and Isola Bella may have suggested to him Kundry's enchanted garden. He may have also been amused, like many other visitors, by standing on a balcony and looking down at the Borromeo motto: "*Umilita, Umilite*" advocating humility. It is sculpted out of box trees and white pebbles in the middle of a green landscape. One only has to contrast the admonition with the splendor of the interior of the castle to fully enjoy the irony.

Alexander Dumas confessed that he had written his worst articles in Stresa, where he spent his time looking at Isola Bella from his window. However, judgments often differed. Stendhal liked Isola Bella on some days but not on others, and wrote: "The divine Borromean Islands seem to me to produce the feeling of beauty to a greater degree than Saint Peter's"; or, speaking of the Palazzo Borromeo: "Contemporary with Versailles, larger for a private individual than Versailles was for a king, but as heartless as Versailles" (Stendhal, *Journal d'Italie*).

The pure Italian baroque palace of the Borromeo family is built in the form of an octagon with three floors surmounted by a dome. Most of the rooms are decorated with friezes of garlands, a motif often used in homes of the Borromeo dynasty. The throne room leads to the library and the state bedroom, in which Napoleon stayed and which still contains the large bed he used. Napoleon spent the day after the Treaty of Campo Formio at Isola Bella and returned twice, once from his headquarters at Mombello and a second time, much later, with Josephine and the French court. Although Napoleon had destroyed their stronghold of Angera, the Borromeos received him so well that he remembered it and later thanked them. At that time, magnificent balls and parties were fashionable. A picture in the room Napoleon occupied then shows one of these receptions during which the diva Grassini, of Milan's La Scala, sang in the gardens. This was one of the great evenings in the history of the palace; for a moment the Borromeos probably forgot that Napoleon was there as a conqueror and that he walked with his generals through the state apartments without perhaps even glancing at the frescoes in the small salon by Francesco Zuccarelli. This painter decorated all the Borromeo palaces including Arona and Senago as well as the castle of Angera which Napoleon had captured some time earlier.

A tour of the palace ends in a long gallery. Among the rather conventional seventeenth- and eighteenth-century paintings in this gallery is a unique work. It consists of a white square marked with evocative shadows which are nothing more than a blurred network of lines left by folding and creasing the canvas. It recalls the modern French painter Yves Klein, who at one of his exhibitions hung an empty frame. The other paintings in the Palazzo Borromeo are overshadowed by this unsigned work.

A subterranean stairway decorated with mirrors leads directly from the gallery in which this painting hangs to the grottoes. A visitor may forget the rooms shown on a tour of the palace, but he will not forget the gardens and the many grottoes, so different from those of Bavarian and Prussian palaces. Baroque volutes form asymmetrical patterns on the walls and ceilings and around the doors, and create a unity of style and a succession of unexpected designs in a long corridor leading to the grottoes. Volutes frame the niches and their seventeenth-century furniture decorated with shells and foliage. The grottoes contain collections of natural marvels—immense black and white pieces of coral arranged as still-life painting with madrepore corals and shells. The juxtaposition of these wonders with Roman busts and the asymmetrical movement of the mural decorations clearly indicate that this is an Italian symphony. Bavarian and German grottoes are darker and contain more curious objects such as rock crystal stalactites, fragments of mirrors or Bayreuth porcelain, and arms extended from the walls holding candelabra. Even in Renaissance grottoes, Rome never accepted magic objects; only shells and pebbles, used for decoration by the ancient Greeks, were permitted.

The garden of the Palazzo Borromeo is its most enchanting gesture. "It looks like nothing but a legendary palace," wrote the French scholar Charles de Brosses. "It is a site worthy of fairies who, one could easily imagine, have brought here a part of the ancient garden of the Hesperides."

The terraced garden, backed against a large stone ornamental façade, is an exercise in baroque bravura and can be seen upon leaving the palace and entering the Court of Diana. It looks like a pyramidal structure with, on the side facing the palace, three tiers of niches decorated with allegorical statues of Lake Maggiore and the four elements. Adorned with fountains, the façade is more than 120 feet high; its top is crowned by the Borromeo unicorn, the family emblem, placed at the highest point of the façade. In the afternoon, a hundred peacocks spread out their tails, fly, and move about the façade; and, every evening, following their natural instinct which assumes the aspect of a rite, they fly up to the unicorn. The first leg of their journey takes them perhaps to the hand of one of the gods on the wide lateral staircases. There they perch for a while before the second leg of their flight takes them to the second terrace, and a third to the unicorn itself. In this way, they abandon the garden and ascend to their night roost.

Each plant in the garden was brought with its earth to Italy by ship. In every age, great gardens have contained exotic varieties of plants, but on Isola Bella ten floors of stone had to be built to contain the earth and plants—always more earth and plants—including the sundew, which must often be replaced because of frost. In May the rhododendrons bloom and flourish on a scale attained only in the gardens of English country homes.

The point of the island is dominated by the mosaic garden, which is in fact an Italian *Jardin d'amour*, with cut trees, sculpted cupids, and statues of the seasons and of Flora. From the western balustrade of the garden can be seen both the shore and ten terraces of the island. Surely it is one of the truly enchanting views of this world.

245. *The cellar of the Palazzo Borromeo is filled with artificial grottoes lined with stones and pebbles.*

246

246. *Prince Vitaliano VI (1620-90) brought Isola Bella to virtual completion.*

247. *Isola Bella, the Palazzo Borromeo.*

247

248. *A mythological god in one of the fountains along the main wall of the garden.*

248

249. *A mythological goddess in a fountain.*

250. *The top of the main wall of the park at Isola Bella.*

251

◁ 251. *Cupids in the Garden of Love.*

256. *Baroque plasterwork and Roman busts differentiate* ▷ *Italian artificial grottoes from their German and French counterparts.*

253. *About 6 P.M. at Isola Bella peacocks alight on statues, trees, or other high points in the garden. Here a peacock rests on the statue of an ancient god before flying off to a higher perch.*

▽

252

253

△

252. *A peacock on the main stairway.*

254. *A peacock at twilight.*

254

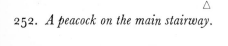

255. *The terrace seen from the rho-* ▷ *dodendron garden.*

255

◁ 257. *A dwarf in eighteenth-century costume at the court of the Borromeos.*

259. *Asymmetrical plasterwork in an artificial grotto.* ▷

257

258. *The baroque vault of a grotto on Isola Bella.* ▽

The Villa Palagonia

An eighteenth-century palace contains statues of monsters, mirrors that distort the human figure, candelabra of cracked teapots, busts made of drinking glasses with broken stems, and chairs studded with spikes so that no one may sit down.

A few miles from Palermo on the coastal road to Messina in Sicily is the site of the eighteenth-century Villa Palagonia, also known as the Palazzo Palagonia. It is a lure for art lovers, especially those attracted by dreams and the fantastic.

Goethe was among the first to report on the villa. In his diary of 1787 he noted: "Elements of the Prince of Palagonia's folly." The prince he referred to was Francesco Ferdinando Gravina, an eccentric and a hunchback. He was one of the strangest figures among the aristocracy of Palermo. Goethe had heard about him and was curious to know more; but he was not the first to walk up the path leading to the palace between two walls crowned with a balustrade decorated with sculpture. An Englishman, Patrick Brydone, preceded him and produced an earlier description of the Prince of Palagonia's villa. Unfortunately, this English physicist was basically a rationalist, and despite his Rousseau-like sensitivity, his description (*A Tour through Sicily and Malta,* 1774) leaves the reader unsatisfied.

Goethe's classical and positive mind was also ill at ease in this imaginary dream-world offered visitors by six hundred statues of five- and six-headed monsters, busts, punchinellos surrounded by serpents, donkeys wearing ties and standing on their hind legs like men, lions dining with napkins tucked under their chins and gulping down oysters, and ostriches in hooped skirts. Incapable of yielding to this disorder, he commented simply: "Human creatures... animals" and added: "a nothing which expects to be taken for something." However, he conscientiously noted that the court of the palace was full of statues intentionally laid on their noses, that the roof was bordered with hydras and monkey musicians, and that an Atlas, traditionally supposed to carry the heavens on his shoulders, had a barrel on his back. Goethe also noted at the palace entrance a dwarf with the head of a Roman emperor crowned with laurel and riding a dolphin, as well as an emperor not crowned with laurel but with thorns and afflicted with two noses. There was clearly something in this affront to nature which escaped Goethe and led him to entitle his notes: "Folly of the Prince of Pala-

260. *The Prince of Palagonia was a hunchback. For narcissistic or ironical reasons, he commissioned a sculptor to make 600 grotesque figures as deformed as he was and adorned the garden, gates, and dependencies of his palace with them. Married to a beautiful wife, the prince hoped to sire a son who would be deformed like himself. Although he succeeded in creating a palace of monsters, he was disappointed in his handsome son.*

gonia." Did he deliberately fail to mention the women with heads of mares, camels, lionesses, and crocodiles intended to represent the four quarters of the world? "Folly"... Goethe probably meant "fantasy." Was this Prince really mad, this Sicilian aristocrat, who belonged to the Order of the Fathers of Mercy, dedicated to ransoming prisoners, and whom Goethe saw begging in the streets of Palermo for money to be used in freeing Sicilians captured by the Barbary pirates? Was he mad like Saint Francis? In his palace a beautiful face is matched by a skull, an infant has the face of an old woman, as in medieval depictions in which the transitory qualities of life were emphasized.

One imagines the inordinate sensitivity of this Sicilian who detected death in every movement. The prince wanted his family of statues to be alive and made them lifelike: of polychrome marble, wearing white wigs, black shoes, red stockings, blue or green clothes, and gold braid. A supreme, yet naïve, symbol is found in a fine statue, which opens and closes its eyes like a doll, and bears a clock on its body, like a cancerous growth. None of these statues, as Patrick Brydone said, resembles things which we see in the heavens, on the earth, or under the water.

The prince was not mad; he was simply Sicilian. In the Piazza Pretoria in Palermo is a fountain decorated with grotesque animals. This expression of the fantastic was typical of the island. In 1787 a young German, Bartels, remarked that the Sicilians "care only for the extraordinary and the marvelous." Even Goethe had to reconsider his conclusion of folly and sought another word to describe the lizards with heads of Chinese dragons and the mythological beasts creeping around the feet of eighteenth-century saints and shepherds. He eventually found nothing better than to coin the term "palagonian," which has since designated the Sicilian love of the fantastic.

The ceilings of the palace, made of strips of rock crystal screwed to slabs of marble, are palagonian. The vaults, covered with mirrors in which the images of guests were distorted, are palagonian, as are the windows of many-tinted glass, which make the world outside look pink, gray, and blue. And how can we otherwise describe busts made of drinking glasses with broken stems and the necks and handles of broken bottles?

The Rouen landscape painter Jean Houël, who spent four years in Sicily between 1771 and 1775, records that in the reception rooms of the Palazzo Palagonia the chairs were arranged in two semicircles in such a way that "people sitting in one semicircle turned their backs on those in the other semicircle." He also remarked that the armchairs sloped forward. Goethe noted that chair legs were unequal in length and, although the chairs were solid enough to inspire confidence in a visitor, iron spikes were

hidden in the velvet cushions of the backs...
Here, certainly, fantasy became folly!

A more recent visitor, the French writer
A. t'Serstevens, who wrote a book on Sicily,
described in detail the residence of the Prince
of Palagonia with horrified fascination and
noted: "The walls of the large reception hall
were covered with the rarest and richest polychrome marble and marble medallions from
which broke loose high-relief family portraits
of the prince, his wife, and other Palagonians
whose clothing, heads, and, above all, arms
emerged by as much as a foot from the frames
in such a manner that the hand of the princess
or her husband seemed extended toward a
visitor who might easily hang his coat on it as
though it were a hook of a coat-rack."

He also referred to the description written
by Patrick Brydone, who had the good fortune
of visiting the villa in its original state, and who
wrote: "All the doors are covered with bits
of glass interspersed with crystal and colored
glass. On either side of the mantel-pieces, in
the recesses of the windows and in the corners
of the rooms were forty obelisks and columns
entirely made of porcelain articles, teapots,
cups, saucers, and chandeliers held together by
cement. One of these columns of coagulated
dishes rests on a huge chamber pot on which
is a stem more than four feet long entirely
made of different sized teapots, the smallest
of which are found near the capital made of

small flower pots arranged in several circles.
The tables could not, of course, resemble ordinary furniture and look like lapis lazuli, porphyry, and chalcedony tombs; other tables are
made of large turtle shells inlaid with gold,
ivory, and mother-of-pearl. The bedroom is
alive with a terrifying zoo of huge snakes,
lizards, spiders, and scorpions sculpted in colored marble."

In the sacristy, a compulsive taste for the
weird is apparent as well as a futile desire to
represent that which cannot be represented.
A bust depicts an exquisitely attired woman
whose face and breasts are being eaten away
by a swarm of scorpions, centipedes, earth-
worms, and moths. A large painted Christ is
fixed horizontally to the ceiling of the chapel;
and into the center of his body has been screwed
a hook from which a kneeling man is suspended
at the end of a chain, floating in air.

Such visitors as Houël and the Comte de
Borch (*Lettres sur la Sicile*, 1787) recognized in
this swinging figure Saint Francis of Assisi, but
Goethe saw in it only the "symbol of the
relentless piety of the Prince." "Zealot," he
wrote and considered it the key to this folly.

This was certainly insanity as far as the
anti-clerical Goethe was concerned. It has been
said that the prince whipped himself, a trait
hardly calculated to persuade Goethe to change
his impression. Others maintain that such flag-
ellation was gossip.

Italy

Goethe met the prince by chance one day while he was engaged in his charitable activities in the streets of Palermo: "He was a tall, thin gentleman, clad in court dress; he moved among the crowd with a calm and dignified air... Curled and powdered, his hat under his arm, in dress clothes, a sword at his side, wearing pretty shoes adorned with jeweled buckles. He was preceded by a servant who offered a silver plate to those passing by."

Brydone described him differently, as "a small, thin man, shivering in the cold wind and apparently afraid of anyone who spoke to him"; Swinburne was similarly uncomplimentary; and Bartels wrote that he only came to life among his monsters.

Monsters were indeed his special infatuation. When his wife was about to give birth, he told anyone who would listen that, if she delivered a real monster, it would be the culminating joy of his life. He stated that the models for his peculiar guests came from Egypt, "where, according to Diodorus, the sun is so strong that it hatches every variety of strange animal from the silt deposited by the Nile." Some claim that the prince was a scientist and devoted his life to the study of monsters. He collected odds and ends, fitting them together according to mysterious laws. He was kind, intelligent, and respected by the peasants for whom he provided work. A contemporary recorded that he spoke to the prince one day at the Viceroy's palace, without realizing who he was, and that he was charmed by the impartial and precise manner in which he discussed everything.

Monsters were expensive, however. The prince was wasting his fortune, and his heirs tried to restrain him. Also, stories abounded and the locale had a frightened air. Pregnant women were afraid of conceiving freaks, and the chief magistrate ordered the prince to destroy his monsters. Destroy his monsters! At this encroachment on his rights, the prince awoke from his lethargy and firmly replied that he was master in his own home, and that those whose eyes were offended had only to keep away.

The king was obliged to intervene. We do not know how the matter was resolved. Some claim that members of the prince's family were placed in charge of his possessions.

261. *A grotesque figure on top of a wall. The Villa Palagonia is now abandoned and tropical vegetation has overgrown the garden. Only the statues high above the ground are still untouched.*

262

262. *Detail of the wall surrounding the park.*

263

263. *A bench against the villa.*

264

264. *Mannerist paintings enframe distorting mirrors with scroll, fruit, and coral motifs.*

265

265. *The polished-marble drawing room is covered with a vaulted ceiling mirrors framed with* trompe-l'œil *paintings. The images of guests refle*

*the mirrors were distorted. In the midst of his courtiers, deformed in their
ections, the prince was not the only hunchback in the room.*

The Chinese Palace in Palermo

Resplendent exile for a king who awaited the fall of an emperor.

In December, 1798, King Ferdinand IV and Queen Maria Carolina of the Kingdom of the Two Sicilies embarked from Naples on Admiral Horatio Nelson's flagship *Vanguard* to sail to Palermo. Fearing that Napoleon's army in Italy might reach Naples, they preferred to wait for quieter days in a safe place.

A few months later, they returned to Naples following the overthrow of the "Parthenopean Republic" established by the French. But in 1806 Ferdinand was again forced to flee to Palermo, Napoleon having placed his brother Joseph Bonaparte and then his brother-in-law Joachim Murat on the throne of Naples. Ferdinand and his family remained in Palermo until 1815, after the fall of Napoleon.

While they were in exile in Sicily, the king and queen, without politics of any significance to occupy their minds, decided to built a folly. Chinoiserie was fashionable, and Ferdinand ordered the construction of a Chinese residence, in which balls would be given and necessary meetings held with his ministers to discuss the future without attaching too much importance to such work. The essential thing was to live as well as possible from day to day, surrounded by a small court and a few friends who thought as he did. Time should at least pass pleasantly since nothing else could be done. For Napoleon, every minute was important to the fulfillment of his ambitions; for Ferdinand IV, the important thing was to while away each minute.

This singular situation gave Palermo a palace not at all in the island's tradition. The royal couple already possessed the ancient palace of the Norman kings there, but it was uncomfortable during warm weather. This made them buy the Villa ai Colli, at the foot of the Monte Pellegrino, from the Baron della Scala. They then commissioned Giuseppe Patricola to build a palace recalling the spirit of the Chinese Pavilion in Brighton. That, however, is the only point of resemblance, for it is essentially an Italian palace in its grace, spirit, and excellent frescoes; the colors are as delicate as they are harsh at Brighton. This is a king's country residence rather than a palace, without any true eccentricities although every detail is curious. In short, this palace is the product of dreams rather than of the bizarre.

A Chinese pagoda had once existed in the garden of the villa acquired by the king, and perhaps this determined the choice of the style of the palace. Patricola was a neoclassical architect, and his preference for this style can be seen in the façade of the palace, as in his use of a colonnade, but he accepted fantasy, painting the walls with red and yellow frescoes, palm trees, and Chinese motifs.

266. *A Chinese palace built in Palermo in the early years of the nineteenth century by the King of the Two Sicilies who had fled Naples threatened by the advance of Napoleon's army.*

Italy

The palace stands behind the iron fence of the garden, every spearhead of which is a Chinese hat with little bells. The tops of the bars are constantly agitated by the wind and the bells never stop ringing. These bells set the stage for our first view of the palace, centered by a curved projection with a pagoda-like roof held up by an Egyptian colonnade. The impression leaves no doubt about the love of fantasy that inspired this now deserted site. Behind the fence is a large garden in which daisies and blue flowers grow profusely. Box trees lining the paths have twisted trunks and apparently were chosen for their shape and capacity to astonish.

Entering the palace, one breathes the atmosphere of the palaces described in Giuseppe Tomasi di Lampedusa's *The Leopard*—innumerable abandoned rooms behind half-closed shutters, shafts of sunlight creating brilliant spots of light on gilded, polychrome, baroque furniture, papered walls and decorations the colors of the sky, blue, orange, and yellow. The vases have been left on the tables, and the chairs are still against the walls in the ballroom or grouped around small pedestal tables in the drawing rooms.

The palace is the sleeping distillation of the past, disturbed only by heavy lace curtains, embroidered with flowers and foliage, flapping against the windows. A ballroom occupies the entire ground floor, painted in the Pompeian style and decorated with engravings of London offered by Nelson to the king. The room next to the ballroom is a copy of a room in the ruins at Pompeii and was used for Cabinet meetings. The ceiling is painted to appear as if it had fallen, allowing one to look at a flight of birds against a painted sky. The king perhaps considered that the simulated disrepair provided an appropriate note of humility to the deliberations which took place in this chamber and at which there was little of importance to discuss. The ballroom placed next to the council chamber and the marble baths clearly indicate the insignificance of politics in the Chinese palace.

The second floor is reached from the ground level by a spiral staircase above which hangs an enormous polyhedral paper lantern dimly lit from the inside. The staircase opens into the dining room, entirely painted in *trompe-l'œil* by G. Patania. A vine-covered trellis and trees in leaf bathe the room in a perpetual green atmosphere. In the center is a still more curious item, a large round table covered with its original cloth and containing round holes through which the dishes filled with food in the basement kitchens were mechanically raised to the table. The king who allegedly spent most of his time making ice-cream and pastry for his guests, put the dishes onto the dumbwaiter below, and Maria Carolina received them in the dining room and returned them to the kitchens by a system of pulleys.

It is difficult to imagine that the continental blockade enabled a court to play at children's dinner parties and the king to become his subjects' pastry-cook. Great military events are always accompanied by a life behind the lines which has little connection with battlefields. Stendhal's novel, *The Charterhouse of Parma*, well proves this point.

The Chinese palace draws from this an oddly amoral additional charm. Its purpose was frivolous, and so was its decoration. But this was a logical product of life in some of the palaces of the Naples region, a number of which are unbearable because of their pomp. A war which was not even theirs gave the king and queen an opportunity to amuse themselves in their colony of Sicily. Palermo was considered African territory, with its palm trees, and arum and papyrus plants. The court opted for pleasure, danced in the cool drawing rooms, and diverted itself with fashionable parlor games. Etiquette was undoubtedly quite formal, but the desire to enjoy life triumphed. The company quickly adapted itself to a perennial succession of amusements, believing that Napoleon was not eternal.

The gaming room, adjoining the dining room, still contains its original furniture. It was decorated by Giuseppe Velásquez of Palermo. Despite its associations, however, it is the most sedate room in the palace.

The king's bedroom close by is arranged in the form of a cross with a Chinese bed in the middle under a canopy shaped like a lotus flower and behind curtains always stirring in the breeze; the room was placed to enjoy a maximum of fresh air. The carved furniture in the room is among the finest examples of the Italian nineteenth-century baroque style. Also included are cast-iron Pompeian consoles and a stool with bowed legs entwined with polychrome snakes and covered with brocaded silk and Directoire trimmings. The painted decorations consist of Louis XV chinoiserie trees filled with birds and arched ceilings adorned with terraces, pagodas, and Chinese figures in *trompe-l'œil*. A caretaker daily fills the vases of this room with wild flowers in memory of the king. A small Chinese drawing room painted in tempera next to the bedroom also has chinoiserie decorations on the walls, as well as a chandelier with crystal palm leaves, Etruscan sofas and tables, and Moorish stools. This mixture of styles recalls English eighteenth-century decorative art, in advance of Italy whose past it was copying.

The king took life lightly and the queen too was frivolous. When over fifty, she still loved, we are told, the seraglio atmosphere of the palace. For the king, his pastry; for the queen, her Turkish delights. The top floor of the palace was shared between the Turkish and Pompeian styles. The queen's apartment was decorated, as she wished, by Patania. One

303

of her Pompeian boudoirs is dedicated to Emma Hamilton, several paintings of whom are hung on the walls. The other boudoir is decorated with fluted columns and medallions containing portraits of the royal children and the king accompanied by symbolic inscriptions such as "My Joy" and "My Hope." This is much more in the tradition of the Italian *mamma* than of the Queen of Naples.

A double spiral staircase leads up to the Turkish Salon, an echo of the follies of Istanbul, with turquoise columns streaked with gold, a silk divan, and an opal chandelier. Through the slats of the shutters can be seen the Palermo countryside and, below the palace, the now wild gardens still encircled by the old box-tree paths running past a fountain overgrown with flowers. The noise of the thousands of little bells tinkling in the wind on the iron grill drifts up to the top of the palace, as does the fragrance of plants, pine trees, arum plants, and cactuses which now invade this tiny Turkish oasis deserted forever after the fall of Napoleon. In the end, the Chinese palace served only to distract an eighteenth-century king from a Romanlike French emperor.

267. *Lord Nelson took the royal family from Naples to* ▷
Palermo on his flagship.

268. *The façade of the palace reflects Chinese and Egyptian influence.*
▽

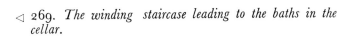

◁ 269. *The winding staircase leading to the baths in the cellar.*

Next pages:
271. *The queen's Turkish salon under the belvedere of the palace.*

272. *The king's chamber leading to the main drawing rooms.*

273. *The family dining room.*

270. *A severely plain architecture for the palace baths.*

271

272

276. *A double stairway led from the queen's* ▷
apartment to the belvedere and the Turkish
salon.

274. *Queen Maria Carolina.*

275. *Ferdinand IV, King of the Two Sicilies.*

274

275

Next pages:
279. Green foliage on the wallpaper at one side of the dining room is lit by a Chinese paper lantern, creating the atmosphere of a cool garden.

280. The Chinese room is decorated with Directoire and Moorish furniture.

278. The ceiling of the room used for council meetings ▷ is decorated with a trompe-l'œil *painting of flying birds.*

277. The king and queen and their family.

The Folly of Rosendael

A castle in the Netherlands celebrated for its gardens.

Haarlem, the Hague, Rotterdam, and Amsterdam are not the whole of Holland. One must go beyond Utrecht and past Arnhem and its delightful gardens to see the parks of Sonsbeek, Klarenbek, and Velp on the banks of the Rhine. One will see as well the park of the castle of Rosendael with its tall trees, small lakes, and waterfalls. A massive thirteenth-century tower preceding the castle contrasts with its park adorned with rococo sculptures and pavilions. Destroyed by fire and again by war, ruined and reburned yet constantly rebuilt between 1412 and 1714, the tower recalls the determination of the counts (later dukes) of Gelderland to win the independence of their county from the Bishop of Utrecht until it fell briefly under Charles the Bold in 1472.

This family of Gelderland played an important role in the history of the Lowlands from the Middle Ages to the Renaissance and married into most of the leading European royal families. Count Reinoud I, the first mentioned in the archives of the castle as having spent time in Rosendael—in the spring of 1314 "from Ascension to Whitsun"—married the widow of King Arthur of Scotland. His son Reinoud II married Eleanor of England, sister of King Edward III and thus acquired many English titles. Reinoud II also succeeded in raising the county to a duchy.

His children were quite violent and seemed to be as ardent in disputing possession of the duchy as in defending it against its exterior enemies. For this reason, Reinoud III, eldest son of Reinoud II, was forced to abdicate in favor of his younger brother Edward after a bitter struggle. Immediately after Edward's death in 1371 a war of succession opened between his heirs, a war which lasted eight years and ended only with the designation of a new duke by the Holy Roman Emperor Charles IV.

In the next century, the family again began to quarrel among itself. Adolf of Gelderland took arms against his father Duke Arnold, and defeated and imprisoned him in a fortress for six years. Beaten by Charles the Bold, Adolf was sent into captivity and his father released.

Along with family quarrels, the Gelders had to support other sieges and combats against their neighbors. However, in 1543, they had to submit to an adversary too powerful for them, the Holy Roman Emperor Charles V, to whom they abandoned sovereignty of the duchy.

During these centuries of combat, the castle experienced fortune and misfortune. Initially a simple hunting lodge located in a pleasant region, it soon became a country house. Next came the addition of a dungeon, which turned

317

The Netherlands

it into a fortress. Destroyed by fire in 1412, the castle was rebuilt, and in 1482 and 1511, it was besieged. The dukes of Gelder were increasingly occupied in waging war and, short of money, allowed the castle gradually to go to ruin in the sixteenth century. It was finally sold to a Dirck van Dorth in 1579.

This was the beginning of a new period for the castle. Entirely rebuilt by its new owners in a beautiful Renaissance style, it was visited by famous guests in the seventeenth century including King William III of England and his wife Mary, the daughter of James II.

In 1714 the interior of the castle was completely destroyed by fire. In 1721 it came into the possession of a new owner, Lubbert Adolf Torck, who married a rich widow, Petronella van Hoorn, and who restored the castle and created its marvelous park, fountains, and grottoes. The shells used for decoration came from the Dutch West Indies, the governor of which was Petronella's father.

The existing castle, built in the eighteenth and nineteenth centuries, contains nothing of note and its architecture is less interesting than its setting. A large dwelling, it consists of a ground floor, two upper stories, and an attic; the windows are framed by ivy, as with many English homes. Its reflection shimmers in water surrounding it and it always looks newly painted.

The great attraction of Rosendael is its park, crossed by a stream with many waterfalls which feed three lakes. A large fountain in the middle of irises is backed by a wall encrusted with shells, some of which are arranged to form enormous daisies or sunflowers. Decorated with eighteenth-century busts and statues, the wall is surmounted by a sundial. This rococo fountain is a long way from the spirit of the Dutch noted for their materialism. "Gold, tobacco, and cheese, these are what they adore," said Claude Saumaise, one of the French scholars attracted by the large salaries of the University of Leiden in the seventeenth century.

Farther on, a flight of a dozen steps diminishing in size and elaborately contrived like a baroque holy-water basin opens upon the sky between two enormous dolphins swimming in the ferns. Everywhere are the sight and sound of rippling water. On one side it flows from a large open shell adorned with stone statuettes, falling in sheets from four fountains guarded by two sea gods. The setting is a mixture of stone, shells, and vegetation, over which the light of Holland, the limpid atmosphere of Vermeer, reigns. Here, more than anywhere else, is the heart of a people who first revealed to Europe the blue porcelain of China and the cashmeres of India, a seafaring people rich in tradition, a people in love with painting and flowers. Rosendael provides a brilliant example of the evolution of the art of gardens as it developed in Western Europe.

282. *The Cascade of Dolphins is enclosed by a wall with niches decorated with shellwork.*

284. An eighteenth-century bust on a fountain in the garden.

285. Beyond the two dolphins stands the castle. ▷ Destroyed by fire, it was later reconstructed. The baroque garden, so different in aspect from the castle, was planned in the eighteenth century.

285

286

◁ 283. Shellwork and stones in the arcade of the wall enclosing the Cascade of Dolphins in front of the castle.

286. A nymph of one of the fountains. ▷

Next pages:
287. A sundial, the pretext for this fountain, overlooks jets of water set among irises.

288. The last fountain in the park is reached over a wooden suspension bridge and features noble sea gods.

The Palace of Fronteira

A Portuguese palace with extraordinary tile decoration.

All Portuguese palaces are decorated with tiles, *azulejos*, but the tiling of the palace of Fronteira near Lisbon is unique. The subjects the tiles depict were chosen by the first Marquis of Fronteira for their symbolic value. They reflect the taste of Portugal since the end of the sixteenth century, from which time the epic poem the *Lusiades* by Luis de Camoëns (1524-80) inspired the Portuguese to cultivate the heroic. Their patriotic sentiments, literature, and arts reflected a longing for grandeur. This is sensed in the first impression at Fronteira with its ceramic portraits of kings posed on galloping horses, in a flourish of plumes and capes—life-sized, mirrored in the calm waters of the large pool.

The small tile panels decorating the low walls around the box-tree parterres depict hundreds of anecdotes, such as noblemen writing at a table in the presence of a masked lady, a monkey standing in front of an organ and conducting singing cats, mermaids clinging at the bottom of the sea to the tail of an ocean king, winged cupids shooting arrows into the sky and scattering flowers, or Venus, a flask of perfume in her hand, followed by a cupid ready to shoot his arrow and seemingly emerging from beds of lilies.

From the King's Gallery a stairway leads down into the garden in which a path on the right leads to a grotto. The terrace of the chapel, over the grotto, is entered through the palace. From the grotto it seems to form part of the park, in which tile decorations abound. The gods of antiquity, Mercury, Diana, and Venus, frame decorated flower-boxes. On the walls are birds with human heads flitting from branch to branch in a symbolic tree; fauns pull chariots and musicians dance. Some panels are dedicated to the glory of the elements. For the sea, there are conch shells; for the earth, fruit. The fires of love are symbolized by tiles reproducing the story of fast women, provocative temptresses, artless and artful procuresses; their accessories are drums, arrows, flowers, clouds, tritons, and wings.

The fairylike palace of Fronteira has no peer. Although less impressive in size than other Portuguese castles, it rivals them because of the surprises which it holds for visitors.

Inside the palace are Portuguese porcelain tiles, such as those in the Hall of Battles which are among the finest in Portugal. One of the scenes depicts the hand-to-hand combat between the Count La Torre and a Spanish general. The palace was inaugurated by the Marquis of Fronteira in 1671 or 1672 in the presence of Peter II, Regent (1667-83) and then King (1683-1706) of Portugal. The dynasty of Braganza, to which Peter belonged, ended

325

289. *Fronteira, a palace decorated with tiles, is near Lisbon. Set into the garden wall are tile panels relating the history of kings and knights. A dual staircase, a portion of which is seen here, leads to a formal garden, a grotto, and the main wing of the palace.*

Portugal

the domination of Spain, following a conspiracy in which Antonio de Mascarenhas, Marquis of Fronteira, played a decisive role. When he received the Regent at the Palace of Fronteira, the marquis concluded the banquet with a theatrical gesture. No mortal was worthy of touching the dishes from which the honored guest had eaten, and they were broken so that they might not be used again. The fragments were set in the pediment of one of the pavilions in the park, since transformed into a chapel, where they can still be seen.

The Dutch tiles in the Portrait Gallery were expressly ordered for the gallery from a noted studio in Flanders. Those of the chapel terrace represent allegorical motifs; nine niches on the terrace contain mythological figures such as Chronos devouring his children, Poetry, and the Arts.

Along with the tiles imported from Flanders, the first Marquis of Fronteira probably also ordered a series of eighty-six tapestries,

which were in the Palace of Chagas but disappeared during the earthquake of 1755. The catastrophe, which surprised the people of Lisbon at an All Saints' Day service and drowned more than six thousand victims in the waters of the Tagus, reduced to dust the palace which the Mascarenhas family owned at Chagas. Following this, the family decided to enlarge the palace at Fronteira.

The palace today belongs to the young Marquis and Marchioness Fernando and Isabel of Fronteira. Their interest lies in philosophy. Descendants of the first marquis, they have added books on the history of contemporary ideas to the large original library. The treasures of the house—the family table service, the eighteenth-century silver-gilt toilet case in Isabel de Fronteira's bedroom, which could well be part of the treasures of the kings of Portugal—are forgotten by the disinterested owners. In the garden, gardeners cut roses. The sun shines on the three-hundred-year-old palace,

290. *Tile panels in a curving wall.*

291. *Scenes on a wall of the palace; in the middle, Triton and his son.*

292. *Musicians and cupids.*

293. *Hunting scenes on the terrace wall.*

294. *A king of Spain in a niche decorated with gold tiles.*

296

296. *The Marquis of Fronteira who built the palace, depicted in bas-relief.*

297

298. *Diana, Goddess of the Hunt.* 298

295. *Exterior gallery of the palace. Ancient statuary recalls antiquity.*

◁ 297. *A grotesque figure painted on tiles.*

299. *A tree of birds with human heads conjures a world in which myth and reality overlap.* ▽

299

POEZIA

Next pages:

302. *A scribe and an attendant with a masked lady.*

303. *A recital of cats conducted by a monkey.*

304. *A wing of the palace of Fronteira made of blue faience complements the blue sky and water.*

◁ 300. *Statues of a young man and a flayed man. Immediately above the bench, an orchestra of cupids.*

301. *The broken fragments of the dishes used by the Regent Peter on his visit to Fronteira are preserved in the pediment of the arch.* ▽

302

EV·SOV·
O MESTRE
DACOLFA

303

304

306. *Chronos devouring his child.*

311

◁ 305. *A geometric garden laid out as a maze.*

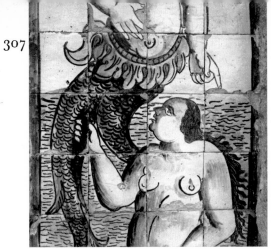

307. *A mermaid and a triton.*

308. *A muse.*

309. *A mermaid.*

310. *Cupids in a field.*

310

306

311. *Venus with a flaming heart in her hand.*

312. *A centurion in the Venus wall.*

312

The Chinoiseries of Drottningholm

Chinese pavilions in a Swedish landscape.

Not far from the royal palace of Drottningholm, six miles from Stockholm, is a site called Kina (China). Adolphus Frederick, King of Sweden, had a Chinese pavilion built there for the thirty-fourth birthday of his wife, Louise-Ulrike von Hohenzollern, celebrated on July 24, 1753. Named Kina Slott, the château of China, it has been replaced by the four pavilions found there today all dating from the 1760's. These are accompanied by an aviary copied, at the queen's desire, from the one built by Prince Henry of Prussia for his residence at Rheinsberg.

The first "China" has its own history. The king had it secretly built in Stockholm and transported on rafts to Drottningholm, where it was assembled to surprise the queen. It had even been arranged that the heir to the throne (the future Gustavus III, who was to drive his mother out of Sweden and to die by an assassin's hand), then seven and disguised in Chinese dress, greeted the queen on the threshold of the pavilion by reciting a welcoming poem and handing her the keys of her new domain on a cushion. Unfortunately, the pavilion collapsed in the winter following its construction due to the combined effect of humidity, snow, and wind. The king decided to replace it by a more spacious and solid structure and enlisted the services of the court architect, Karl Frederick Adelcrantz. He created the Chinese pavilion and three small pavilions now on the Kina site. Johann Erich Rehn and the painter Johann Pasch were responsible for the decoration. The Chinese pavilion had been finished a number of years when it was inaugurated in 1770 with a Chinese party as brilliant as any fête celebrated in the great capitals of Europe.

China and the taste for chinoiserie thus became firmly entrenched in Sweden after arriving via Germany, where Versailles and Paris set the tone for fashion. Chinoiserie had been brought there by Johann Franz Oeben, who was born in Franconia and as a young man had gone to Paris where he was welcomed by his compatriot Jean Henri Riesener, with whom he had made a roll-top desk for Louis XV that became a famous example of the cabinet-maker's art. Quick to exploit the whims of fashion, Oeben and Riesener learned to use the red, gold, and black polychrome of Chinese lacquer. The Company of the Indies sent back to Paris from the East new woods, including bird's-eye mahogany, to which the bright colors of exotic subjects could be applied. The vogue derived from the Chinese Closet (1690) of Monsieur, Louis XIV's brother, for his château in Saint-Cloud. This had been followed by a similar room at the Trianon, one in Versailles,

337

one in Berlin in Frederick II's palace, and one in Drottningholm.

In fact, the chinoiserie style was created in England, and Chinese pavilions, pagodas, and gardens which the English called "Chinese" and which the French called "English" were soon found in Vienna at Schoenbrunn, in Bavaria, and in France. Louis XIV erected the Porcelain Pavilion, now destroyed but once a celebrated feature of the gardens of Versailles. Thereafter albums, some of which were fantastic and others scholarly, disseminated information on the architecture of China through plans and tint drawings. An outstanding example was the album of Sir William Chambers, who designed the Kew Palace Pagoda in England. Wallpaper representing scenes of Chinese life and Chinese gardens filled with birds, flowers, and insects the names of which were completely unknown soon covered the walls of fashionable homes.

Rehn and Pasch, in the forefront of European fashion, imposed Chinese decoration on a rococo background in the pavilions of Drottningholm. White Chinese figures from the Kang-hsi period (1662-1722), placed on small gilt wood rococo consoles, and engravings of birds and exotic plants, give an intimate touch to the small drawing room in Kina Slott with its echoes of Versailles and Peking. In the hall, paved with black and white marble and sparkling with Bohemian crystal, are two large gilt bronze vases, from which festoon gilt bronze branches framing the French window opening on the park. In the turquoise drawing room, decorated by Pasch but inspired by François Boucher, two Louis XVI chairs made in Sweden guard a large China vase, which Louise Ulrike ordered from the Company of the Indies.

The red drawing room strongly resembles one of the Chinese drawing rooms of the Pagodenburg pavilion of the Nymphenburg in Munich. Red painted woodwork, accented by gilded relievo, frames black and gold Chinese lacquer panels; statuettes stand on eighteenth-century gilded wooden console tables; the stools and Louis XV chairs are upholstered in coral red satin; and several black lacquer cabinets contain collections of Chinese porcelain figures.

The pink drawing room is similar in spirit to the red drawing room but much less formal and quite closely related to the descriptions of drawing rooms conceived by M. de Monville for the truncated column of the Desert of Retz in France. This drawing room at Drottningholm is paneled in pink woodwork with gilded moldings. The panels are decorated with Chinese motifs on a light background. The Louis XV chairs are upholstered in eighteenth-century chintz ornamented by Chinese motifs on a light background. Against the walls, on top of gilded consoles, as in the other drawing rooms, and on the mantels above the fireplaces are tall, eighteenth-century Chinese polychrome statuettes and, in the spirit of the seventeenth century, large blue Chinese vases at some of the windows. Vases also stand on the gilded console tables in the corners of the drawing room. The white fire screen is embroidered with pastel flowers. The light in this small pink drawing room makes it more a folly for intimacy than one for dazzling or astonishing. Other drawing rooms have emerald woodwork, immense mirrors, and nearly full-sized human figures dressed in Chinese costumes, but are no longer furnished.

One of the corner pavilions houses the dining room which was once very well furnished; some of the furniture in this room rose up out of the floor as at the castle of Linderhof of Ludwig II of Bavaria. Peach and other fruit trees surround all of these Chinese follies. They are quite far removed from Drottningholm castle, which is sumptuous and severe, and seems to have played exactly the same role at this official royal residence as the Petit Trianon in Versailles. The pavilions offered a place where pomp and ceremony could be forgotten if only for a few hours: "One leads an odd sort of life here, with court entertainments alternating with rural pleasures," wrote a duchess in 1777 to one of her friends. "If the weather is bad, one stays in the palace. At Kina, simple dresses for the women; frock-coat or country clothes for the men..."

In 1781, ten years after the death of Adolphus Frederick, Gustavus, who was king,

thought it wise to place his mother's dream world under the protection of guards. He acted with tact. Adelcrantz, the court architect, had the idea of a building for a guard house which would imitate a Turkish tent and blend into the exotic architectural complex.

Shortly afterward, at the palace at Haga, the architect Piper erected two similar structures, which reflected a fashion for things Turkish emanating from France via Germany. These tents made of metal recall the reproduction of Ottoman tents used by kings for large receptions in the sixteenth and seventeenth centuries. The two large tents are decorated in several colors; one is blue and the other striped. One is used as the entrance to the park of Haga, now open to the public. Painted in *trompe-l'œil*, the tents were decorated with simulated fringes, braid, and drapes.

Did Gustavus III really want to protect the treasures of Kina Slott or was it simply to keep an eye on his tiresome mother, whom he was about to drive out of Drottningholm? The French Revolution had hardened him. He had reduced the rights of the Swedish nobility, been reconciled with Russia, and was about to intervene against the French Revolution when one of his officers came up to him at a masked ball and, according to Verdi, who made this the subject of his opera *A Masked Ball*, addressed him as "Good evening, beautiful mask," and assassinated him.

339

Sweden

Twenty years later, Kina received a visit from one of the prettiest women of the nineteenth century, Désirée Clary, sister-in-law of Joseph Bonaparte and wife of Jean Bernadotte, called Sergeant Belle Jambe. He became a Marshal of the French Empire and Prince of Pontecorvo and was elected a royal prince of Sweden by the Swedish Diet in 1810. The son of Gustavus III had shown himself incapable of ruling and was deposed; his uncle Charles XIII had succeeded him. Thinking it expedient to place on the throne a relation of Napoleon, the Diet forced the king to accept a former French corporal as the heir to the crown of Sweden. In September, 1810, Bernadotte was ushered into the king's presence in the royal palace of Drottningholm, where he knelt before him and addressed him as "my father." The beautiful Désirée Clary thus became Queen of Sweden. But the chinoiseries of Drottningholm could not keep her far from Paris. After a short time in Sweden, she returned to France leaving her son, the young Oscar, with her husband. Both were to be kings of Sweden and Norway.

314. *The main façade of the Chinese pavilion with a pagoda-like roof, green doors, and eighteenth-century Chinese pilasters.*

Next pages:

318. *The pink drawing room of the Chinese pavilion. Chinese brocade on the walls and chairs. Chinese vases and porcelain statues.*

319. *Black and red lacquer and porcelain figurines integrated with rococo furnishings.*

320. *The entrance hall of the Chinese pavilion leads to a small drawing room.*

321. *An annex building of the Chinese pavilion seen from a balcony.*

322. *A small Chinese gazebo in a wild garden.*

323. *The main entrance to the Chinese pavilion is decorated with marble and bas-reliefs.*

316. *Gustavus III (1746-92), King of Sweden.*

317. *One of the small pavilions.*

◁ 315. *The Chinese pavilion has wings connecting annex structures.*

318

319

320

321

322

325

326

325. *Fireplace in the Chinese pavil-ion decorated with Chinese statuettes.*

326. *The blue and green salon.*

327. *Detail of the pink salon.*

327

◁ 324. *A tent made of metal was erected for the guards of the Chinese pavilion.*

328

330. *The dining room at Haga.*

329

329. *Gustavus III's library at Haga.*

◁ 328. *The eighteenth-century palace at Haga near Stockholm.*

331. *The main drawing room of Haga overlooks a pond.*

Next page:
334. *A circular gazebo in an idyllic landscape for Gustavus III, who was to die assassinated at a masked ball.*

332

332. *A metal tent painted with* trompe-l'œil *near the palace at Haga is similar to the tent at Drottningholm.*

333. *A large Turkish tent made of metal conjures up* ▷ *the illusion of the Ottoman Empire despite the crown of the Kings of Sweden on its roof.*

333

ACKNOWLEDGMENTS AND INDEX

Acknowledgments

The author wishes to express appreciation to the following for their aid in the preparation of this book :

The curator of the château of Bayreuth.
The curator of the château of Linderhof.
The curator of the château of Hohenschwangau.
The curator of the château of Neuschwanstein.
The curator of the château of Herrenchiemsee.
The curator of the château of Nymphenburg.
The curator of the château of Schwetzingen.
The curator of the Royal Pavilion at Brighton.
The curator of the château of Ambras.
The curator of the château of Hellbrunn.
J. Démaret, chief architect of the French government.
The curator of the château of Rambouillet.
The curator of the château of Versailles.
The curator of the palace of Bomarzo.
The curator of the palace of Caserta.
The curator of the palace of Palagonia.
The curator of the Chinese palace of Palermo.
The curator of the château of Rosendael.
The curator of the château of Drottningholm.
The curator of the château of Haga.

Special thanks are due to :

Daniel Apert, who aided in the literary documentation of the book.
The Prince Borromeo, who has graciously authorized the documentation on the palace of Isola Bella.
Rainer von Diez, who has permitted publication of his residence while still in course of completion.
Monsieur Maurice Eschapasse, curator of Historic Monuments, whose aid and goodwill have been exceptional in the preparation of this book.
The Marquis and Marchioness Fernando and Isabel de Fronteira, who so graciously opened their residence.
Marc Garland, who through his extensive knowledge of rare objects and of the châteaux of Austria and Bavaria was of immense aid in researching the volume.
The Vicomtesse Françoise d'Harcourt, whose knowledge of the life of Beckford and of Fonthill Abbey aided in the publication of the history of that strange house.
Professor Jacques Lamb for his valuable insights into the role of dreams in reality.
Mademoiselle Bénédicte Pesle and the Galerie Iolas for their aid in the realization of the chapter on the Bird's Dream.
The Count Hélie de Pourtalès, who graciously provided family mementos from his residence, one of the last Parisian follies erected in the belle époque.
The Baron Alexis de Rede, who permitted consultation of his library of books on architectural marvels.

Madame Niki de Saint-Phalle, who created the sculptures of the Bird's Dream, undoubtedly the unique contemporary fantastic residence.

The Countess Ernestina von Schönborn and her son Karl von Schönborn-Wiesentheid, who willingly opened their residence, the château of Pommersfelden.

The pictures of the castles of Ludwig II of Bavaria, the Nymphenburg, Brighton, Ambras, Hellbrunn, the Shell Cottage and Dairy at Rambouillet, the palace of Palagonia, and the Chinese palace of Palermo were realized by Claude Arthaud with the collaboration of the studio of RICHARD ET BLIN (assistant operator JACQUES VAINSTAIN).

The other photographs are by :

ÉDITIONS ARTHAUD : M. Audrain : 238, 241, 242; P. Dubure : 189, 226 (Musée du Louvre, Cabinet Rothschild, Collection Soulavie); H. Paillasson : 220, 222, 223; Trincano : 219.

AVANT-SCÈNE DU CINÉMA, Paris : 163.

BIBLIOTHÈQUE NATIONALE, Paris : 187, 191, 193, 194.

BLINKHORNS, Banbury, England : 103 (Collection Bearsted, Upton House, Banbury).

BRITISH MUSEUM, London : 101, 102, 105, 106.

BULLOZ, Paris : 104 (Musée de Montpellier), 178 (Bibliothèque Nationale, Paris).

PRIVATE COLLECTIONS : 164, 235.

CONNAISSANCE DES ARTS, Paris : 107, 109, 111, 113, 180 (Collection The Antique Porcelain, London), 304 (color), 181 (Millet, Musée de Sèvres), 183 (R. Guillemot), 217 and 218 (J. Guillot, Bibliothèque Nationale, Paris).

LONGANESI EDITORE, Milano : 99 (from *La filosofia dell'arredamento*).

GIRAUDON, Paris : 108, 119 (Germälde Kaser Galerie, Vienna), 177, 221 (Collection Clark), 224 (Bibliothèque Nationale, Paris), 274 and 277 (Musée Condé, Chantilly), 275 (Musée de Versailles).

SAN SIMEON STATE MONUMENT, San Simeon, California : 162, 167.

KUNGL. BIBLIOTEKET, Stockholm : 316.

W. LENGEMANN, Kassel : 200.

METROPOLITAN MUSEUM OF ART, New York : 110, 112.

MUSEUM OF MODERN ART, Stockholm : 199, 203.

NATIONAL MUSEUM, Stockholm : 188, 192, 225.

ROYAL PAVILION, Brighton : 91, 92, 96.

ASSOCIATION OF NATIONAL MUSEUMS AND CHÂTEAUX OF BAVARIA, Munich : 18.

RÉUNION DES MUSÉES NATIONAUX, Versailles : 114, 207 to 216.

ROGER-VIOLLET, Paris : 267.

A. SAILER, " Bayerns Märchenkönig, " Verlag Bruckmann, Munich : 17, 19, 20, 21, 29, 31, 32, 33, 34, 43, 44, 45, 46.

E. SCHMIED, Hamburg : 196.

Index

This volume was produced
under the supervision of Claude Arthaud.
Monochrome photogravure by Braun and C°, Mulhouse.
Four-color offset by La Photolith, Paris.
Text printed by l'Imprimerie Floch, Mayenne.
« Chromomat » gravure and coated papers
from Arjomari-Prioux, Paris.
Four-color offset films by Dupont, Charenton-le-Pont.
Binding by l'Atelier du Livre, Châtillon-sous-Bagneux.
Cloth from Texlibris, Paris.
Printed in France.
26-4-73 — N° 11837